3/17/24

Ross Cotton Young

Chris —
   Thanks for all the
"Wonderful" productions of our
SKC Newsletter - and most of all
for the fabulous friendship.   Margret

Ross "Cotton" Young, 1951

L*if*elong Looper

The Story of a Caddie Legend

CINDY O'KREPKI

Lifelong Looper ~ The Story of a Caddie Legend
Casebound Edition

Copyright © 2005 BlueStreak Publishing LLC

Jacket design by Timothy Kling
Layout & Design: Peter O'Krepki

Published by BlueStreak Publishing LLC
USA

ISBN 0-9772379-0-7

www.BlueStreakPublishing.com
www.LifelongLooper.com

Printed in the United States of America

October 2005

May this book dedicated to my grandfather
and caddie champion, Ross "Cotton" Young
be a fitting tribute to a man who
dedicated his life to the greatest of games.

And may it serve as a parable for
all those who think the mundane tasks
of service performed every day by
ordinary people can't add up to a legacy.

"The first thing to understand about caddying is that it's not brain surgery. It is more complicated than that."
                                                        —*Lawrence Donegan*

"Make friends with your caddie and the game will make friends with you."   —*Stephen Potter*

"Golf is, in part, a game; but only in part. It is also a religion, a fever, a vice, a mirage, a frenzy, an abscess, a joy, a thrill, a pest, a disease, an uplift, a brooding melancholy, a dream of yesterday, a disappointing today and a hope for tomorrow."
                                                        —*Grantland Rice*

"Everyone has the power for greatness—not for fame but greatness, because greatness is determined by service."
                                        —*Dr. Martin Luther King Jr.*

Golfer: "Think I'm going to drown myself in the lake."
Caddie: "Think you can keep your head down that long?"

Golfer: "I'd move heaven and earth to break 100 on this
course."
Caddie: "Try heaven, you've already moved most of the
earth."

Golfer: "Please stop checking your watch all the time. It's
too much of a distraction."
Caddie: "It's not a watch—it's a compass."

Golfer: "Do you think my game is improving?"
Caddie: "Yes sir, you miss the ball much closer now."

Golfer: "You've got to be the worst caddie in the world."
Caddie: "I don't think so, sir. That would be too much of
a coincidence."

The jokes contained on this page are of unknown origin
—passed on to Cotton by one of his players. I'd wager that
they were written by a caddie, wouldn't you?

Contents

Foreword

With the spotlight so often on the stars who tour and win great sums of money in the world of golf, it is the aim of the Professional Caddies Association (PCA) to honor those who read the greens, carry the bags and share the wisdom that sinks birdies, escapes bunkers and supports champions. The First Annual Professional Caddies Association Worldwide Caddie Hall of Fame ceremony was held on March 19, 2000 at the World Golf Village Renaissance Hotel in Florida. This ceremony ushered in not only a new millennium, but also a new level of recognition for caddies and their unique and invaluable contributions to the game of golf.

At this inaugural ceremony, the PCA was proud to honor Ross "Cotton" Young, the longest-working caddie in history, and a man we will never forget. His longevity is certainly notable, but even greater is his heart. Though Cotton has been caddying since 1929 and knows everything about the fairways of the Saucon Valley Country Club in Bethlehem, PA, he still maintains the "Three-Up" caddie motto: "Show up, keep up, and shut up." His other golden rule is to give advice only when asked.

One of my favorite stories contained in this book is when Cotton caddied for Jerry Barber in the 1992 U.S. Open. Barber informed Cotton "that he did not need any advice reading the greens." Maintaining his golden rule, Cotton respectfully withheld this advice, and those who watched the tournament now convey with a chuckle, "Barber missed many putts as a result."

Cotton Young will always be one of the great caddies of all time. He is honored and respected by peers and players, employers and friends—he is a person who will carry the banner for all caddies worldwide. His life story will appeal not just to all who love golf—but also to all who appreciate a life well lived. Cotton is an inspiration; a grand example of, "If you love what you do, you'll never work a day in your life." The Professional Caddies Association recommends *Lifelong Looper* as a unique book that shines a light on the honorable profession of caddying and a man, Cotton Young, who honored the sport of golf through his service.

Dennis M. Cone
Founder, PCA Worldwide Foundation

Preface

Have you ever known someone your entire life only to realize that you barely knew them at all? I have had such an experience with my own grandfather, Ross "Cotton" Young. Until recently, I only knew him as my grandfather, the senior patriarch presiding over four generations of heirs—a gentle man whose loving kindness was expressed mostly in facial expressions and quiet companionship.

His presence in the world is something I always took for granted—that is, until he suffered a stroke. This unfortunate event drew my attention to the professional man and to the realization that I knew relatively little about his adult life. What I learned was so wonderful that I set out to share the joy and value in a life which chronicles an American era that appears to be fading into history, but not completely. The traditions and beliefs that guide my grandfather's life and those he serves are still alive. They are safely guarded, practiced and taught on tee boxes and in clubhouses all over America. This is a story about one man's fascinating life of 77 years on the bag, guiding countless members and guests on a golf course against a backdrop of history that beckons to be remembered and cherished by golfers and the rest of us for generations to come.

Cotton was always a hero to me. Not because of

his status as a much sought-after caddie or because of the notable men and women for whom he caddied, but because of the time we spent together.

I remember our many trips to a local amusement park, his reckless abandon to the sliding board in our swimming pool, the way he floated effortlessly on his back in the ocean—oblivious to the world around him. I especially remember his masterful whistling of a complex tune.

The earliest, fondest memory of my grandfather is the way his eyes lit up as he smiled when I entered the room. Today, when whispering into his great and great, great grandchildren's ears, his eyes still dance with a tender twinkle of anticipation at what they might say or do. My grandfather's earliest memory of me is my premature entry into the world, barely tipping the scales at just three pounds. So fragile and tiny, even swaddled in a baby blanket, I could comfortably fit inside a shoe box, and as if afraid to break me, I'm told he refused to hold me for the longest time.

One could say that Cotton lived a double life of sorts, one at home and one at the Saucon Valley Country Club in Bethlehem, PA. It is likely that we, his family, never fully understood the depth of his life, work ethic or the near "celebrity" of his country club world.

In his family setting, Cotton was a quiet, private man, busying himself with the cares of life and the needs of others, never particularly concerned with making his own needs or dreams known. To his family, he was famous for his brevity in speech (save for the subject of golf). Cotton is somewhat of a paradox. He's demure about the spotlight, yet whenever given the opportunity to share his experiences as a caddie, he showcases a charisma unique to those who possess magnetism but seem unaware of the gift.

For years he observed men and women from all walks of life and it was obvious to all that Cotton's love for the game was surpassed only by his love for the people who played the game. This combination of people and golf was so sublimely satisfying that he spent a lifetime helping to bring the two together. Anyone who knows Cotton understands that he has always been a man who lives and breathes to caddie.

We may all be guilty of loosely throwing the word legend around. Cotton's 77 years of caddying should inarguably put him in that category. He wasn't looking for a legacy or to be a legend, but once he got a bag on his shoulders, it was there for good. One visit to his beloved Saucon Valley Country Club and I was intrigued, wondering what it was like to be part of the fabric of a country club, to spend a lifetime caddying on its great courses, to know it and its members so intimately, so thoroughly, to see it day after day, until days become seasons, the seasons years, and the years a lifetime. What was the spirit— the ethos, the sights and sounds of Saucon? While writing this book, I spent many a day taking in the rich beauty of Cotton's work environment, immersing myself in Saucon's storied golf holes, interviewing staff members, caddies and players, smelling the unmistakable, earthy scent of freshly mown grass. My inquisitive foray led me to the conclusion that unless one has put his whole mind and heart into working the greens, understanding the soul of a lifelong caddie is easier said than done.

Many underestimate career caddies in general, and Cotton in particular. In fact, when people first meet Cotton, they think they know what they are getting. But they are usually wrong...as was I. And if you had a desire to have a sit-down, in-depth conversation with him, you might still be waiting. While tracking my grandfather's path through the past for the writing of *Lifelong Looper*, Cotton's succinct replies to my inquiries only heightened the mysteries I found so alluring. I discovered that my grandfather, like the subtle undulations of his beloved Old Course, could be read if only you knew how to read him. It would be easy to misjudge this seeming lack of profundity, but I've come to discover that gold is hidden in the mines of Cotton's life and it is appreciated most by those who recognize its value. I didn't begin to recognize fully the treasures of my grandfather until his 2000 induction into the Professional Caddies Association Worldwide Hall of Fame in St. Augustine, Florida. That momentous event inspired my process of documenting his life. The years reveal an ordinary man who found the secret to living an extraordinary life through honor, humility and service to others.

Cotton's story begins when golf clubs were hickory shafts and a caddie's hourly rate was 20 cents. He walked more than 10,000 loops over the course of his career. That's more than 60,000 miles of green fairways—equivalent to two and a half times around the world! Back in the day, he was energized by such activity, but now his hair is gray, his face is wizened, and he is tired. Many seasons have passed, taking with them his youth. What is left behind and will always remain, however, are the fascinating life experiences contained in this book.

And when Cotton smiles, it still reaches his eyes.

Cindy O'Krepki

The Course is Set

FOLLOWING THE GOLF BALL and its unpredictable journey from tee to pin isn't for the weak or fainthearted. Poor coordination, lack of stamina, erratic biorhythms, and an unruly mind are just a few of the obstacles to hitting a pure shot. Add to that the smallest ball in sport, with a 5.28-inch circumference, weighing 1.6 ounces must find its way *off* of a two-inch angled surface to and then *in* a far-off hole with only a 4.25-inch diameter. Golf with all of its disappointments, anxieties, absurdities and cruel twists of fate creates the need for an ally—one to share the common goal of every player—to sink the little ball in the little hole with the long slender stick in the fewest strokes. Considering all the factors that go into driving the ball well, hitting greens and sinking putts, every golfer could use a companion to guide, cajole, counsel, humor and inspire. Thus, the call of the caddie.

If ever a man was to the fairway born, it was Ross "Cotton" Young. For most of his 89 years, he has lived and breathed golf and has loved every minute of it. All caddies learn the game, but not all master the craft. As a lifelong looper, Cotton's expertise on the bag is legendary.

An observer of thousands of golf swings, Cotton answered his players' endless pursuits of swing analysis and exploration, freely offering tips to anyone who asked. He demystified the golf swing's complexities with his straightforward suggestions on how to adjust a swing to create pure contact with the clubface. Cotton's players would often be surprised when the outcome was a longer, more accurate drive.

This is a man who possessed an instinctive understanding of what made his players tick. Cotton offered encouragement and imparted habits of thought to overcome phobias, leading his players to reach new heights they may not have attained on their own. He could help to restore players' insidious crises of confidence in their short game with the skill of a sports psychologist, long before the occupation ever existed.

Cotton knew intuitively where a ball was likely to land just by the sound of it propelling off the club head, and rarely lost a Titleist in the line of duty. He's been known to say, "The ball in flight doesn't lie." With amazing accuracy, this ace of caddies could predict if the dimpled sphere would bear to the right or to the left or fly high in the air or hug low to the ground.

Cotton helped his golfers to escape the precarious greenside dilemmas lining the course. He saw a player's line as distinctly as if he had snapped it with a chalky carpenter's string, having every nuance of the course indelibly marked in the recesses of his mind. With pinpoint precision, Cotton knew how far you could hit, how far to the green and what club you should use after he saw you play just one hole. A master of yardage and club selection, Cotton, to his players' amazement, handed them the perfect club from his bag of tricks time after time, and then coaxed a shot out of them they didn't know they were capable of hitting.

Strapping on a bag has been a way of life for Cotton, now in his 77th year at the Saucon Valley Country Club. What would possess a man to become a lifelong looper? It's not one single thing but the collection of experiences, large and small, that comprise Cotton's intoxicating passion for the game and his profession. Here's how it all began.

Ross "Cotton" Young, a time capsule of a man, was born on October 18, 1915, two years before the U.S. declared war on Germany in World War I. In this capsule are vivid reminiscences spanning from the abject poverty of the Great Depression to the devastating attack on Pearl Harbor, from the uniting of a nation to win the fight on Nazi fascism in World War II to the fall of the Twin Towers from the proud New York skyline. Cotton's life is crafted by his collection of memories and the experiences birthed from both seasons of despair and triumph.

His years spanned the Industrial Age that spawned America's amazing rise to superpower status and the modern marvels of the Information Age. Cotton watched, as the world did, the invention of the first "iron horse"—the Model A automobile—and later, the first assembly line car, the Model T Ford called the "Tin Lizzie."

"Imagine how I felt when I first heard someone on the other end of a telephone," Cotton exclaims. "I didn't even own a telephone until I was 34 years old, a television until I was 37 and a car until I was 45. We walked everywhere we went," he explains. "It's all we knew." A sudden flash of sobriety appears in Cotton's twinkling eyes as he is struck by how dramatically life has changed over the span of almost a century.

It wasn't likely that Cotton would ever become acquainted with the royal and ancient game of golf and the manicured emerald of the greens. His father, Horace Young, was a loom fixer and patriarch of 13 children who had little means and no time for leisure sport. Horace never taught his son golf, but he *did* teach him a work ethic that would, in time, shape his son's future.

Cotton's father, Horace, was a stern disciplinarian who held puritanically rigid ideas of right and wrong. He taught his children the straight and narrow of life, relentlessly instilling in them the proper respect for others. Boorish or disrespectful behavior was rewarded by "a board to the backside," Cotton says, wide-eyed and nodding, his face still reflecting the awe of his childhood discipline. It says something about the place and time of his youth—a far cry from present-day family dynamics. With "politically correct" parenting nearly a century away, Horace, Sr.'s unwavering principles would likely be viewed as extreme or harsh today. Right was right and wrong was wrong, no matter what shades of gray anyone else seemed to see. Hard work and humility were core principles Cotton learned from this man named Horace, though his years of knowing him were all too brief.

The people in the little town of Bethlehem, Pennsylvania where Cotton was born valued traditional ways. Everyone knew everybody else. Children usually married someone from their hometown or a neighboring one; then they would settle down nearby and raise a family. Few ever traveled far from home.

In the so-called good ole days, medical care was much less sophisticated and life spans were much shorter. Horace and his wife, Lottie, faced the tragedy of not just one, but three of their children dying during a diphtheria epidemic that stole many lives before the advent of certain vaccines. During the 1920s, diphtheria was the leading cause of death among infants and children. The greatly feared disease struck some 150,000 people a year and killed about 15,000. In this era, most families had a large number of children, knowing they were likely to lose one or two. Though few parents escaped this painful loss, knowing they were not alone was little consolation. The death of a child was an extremely difficult experience, yet it rarely brought families to more than a temporary halt.

Most of the homes in their part of town were weathered by age and rather small by the standards of today. The Young home was a lively place with

10 active young and adolescent children. The family of 12 lived in a three-story, three-bedroom whitewashed home on a dirt road named Benner Avenue. Cotton and one of his brothers bunked in the third-floor attic. This house was home for Cotton until he married in 1937.

In this current age of personal computers and digital video, how incapacitated would we be if, all in one day, our computer crashed, our electricity went off, our phone went dead, our car was towed and our indoor plumbing ceased? But this was simply a way of life for Cotton, whose only exposure to running water as a youth was the steady flow through the attic roof when it rained. State-of-the-art equipment was a hand-pump used to prime cold water from the cistern below the trap door in the kitchen. Foods were stored in an icebox and kept cold with a 10-cent, 24-pound ice block delivered to the Young home several times a week. A drip pan underneath caught the water from the melting ice.

Since there was no electricity, oil lamps placed in just a few rooms were the sole source of light after the sun went down. "We got a lot more sleep in those days. There wasn't much to do after dark," Cotton remarks. Heat was provided by a coal-burning stove in the kitchen and a potbelly stove in the living room with a hole cut in the ceiling to allow the heat to rise to the second floor.

Cotton's attic bedroom was unbearably hot in summer and freezing cold in winter. Over time the slate roof succumbed to the elements, leaving the brothers to strategically place pails to catch the dripping water. Even today, the memory of winters' past makes Cotton shiver. The three boys slept in scratchy woolen long johns, layered in blankets and topped off with sheepskin throws. "It was times like those when I made a vow. When I married and had a family of my own, we'd never be cold," says Cotton. To this day, when you visit Cotton's home, the thermostat is always set higher than what most people would consider comfortable.

His childhood home was sparsely decorated, the most striking interior feature being the royal blue booth in the kitchen that seated only six at a time. To make do, the 12-member Young family ate their meals in shifts. "Times haven't changed too much as far as everyone gathering in the kitchen," Cotton notes. "It was always our favorite and sometimes the only warm room in the house."

Perhaps more shocking by today's standards was that 11 people (by this time, Cotton's oldest brother had enlisted in the Navy) could harmoniously co-exist with just one bathroom. This one room relief center was a backyard outhouse and "honey-dippers" would come around once a year to clean it. Cotton notes with characteristic bemusement the irony of their job title and how the family would eagerly await their yearly shipment of toilet paper—the Sears and Roebuck catalog. "When the catalog supply ran low, we substituted paper wrappers used to pack oranges," Cotton guffaws.

"We only took a bath once a week," remembers Cotton. Water was heated in a big copper pot to fill a makeshift galvanized tub, which was huge and round and placed in the kitchen. Seniority dictated the bathing order, from the oldest down to the youngest— a common practice at the time. By the end of this nine-child ritual, the water was filthy, which gave rise to the phrase, "Don't throw the baby out with the bath water."

Without computer games or TV to captivate them, the children's summertime playground was the Lehigh River. This was where a mischievous pack of boys first gave tow-headed Ross his nickname of "Cotton." Even dripping wet, his tangled (despite his mother's best attempts) mop of blonde hair seemed the color of the purist and whitest cotton. And the rest, as they say, is history.

Back then, a good childhood wasn't measured by how nurtured you were, but by mere survival. A parent's greatest challenge was simply providing a roof for cover and food for nourishment, yet Cotton's mother, Lottie, also provided a warm and caring influence. Cotton still clings to the sweet memory of his favorite childhood treat—his mother's homemade donuts. When he claims, "I've never had another donut like it," some might wonder if he ever tried a Krispy Kreme, but it's likely that no recipe could come close to the loving memories attached to those donuts.

In their small, fenced-in backyard, Lottie kept chickens, which produced a steady supply of fresh eggs. Children were expected to grow up faster than modern day children and contributed to household tasks as early as five or six. Part of Cotton's daily chores included gathering the eggs and cleaning out the chicken coop. Poultry was reserved for holiday meals or other special occasions when Cotton would help his mother butcher and pluck the home-raised chickens. "You never tasted chicken so good," he says.

When Cotton reflects on Lottie, he recalls, "In some ways she was Dad's opposite." Where Horace was austere strength and discipline, his wife was softness and warmth. His father's hard work and no play discipline were in direct contrast to the comfort she brought to the home—a comfort that was soon to be sorely needed.

It was an ordinary Sunday afternoon at the Young household until, without warning, Cotton's father clutched his chest and fell to the floor. Though Lottie, for the sake of the children, attempted to downplay the collapse, she still sent Cotton to fetch the doctor. As fast as any 13-year-old boy could, he ran down two miles of a sleepy, unpaved road to what was known as Five Points to find Dr. Deck. As he ran, emotions washed over him, with memories and fears alternately vying for his attention. Heaving, he burst through the door and spilled out the series of events in a tumble of words. Seemingly unmoved, Dr. Deck assured the boy that he would be along as soon as he possibly could. This was small comfort, but having no recourse, Cotton headed for home, attempting to keep his fears at bay. As children often do, this young boy perceived his father to be invincible. Anything else was unthinkable. Looking for evidence that his father would be fine, Cotton caught his breath and went to his parent's bedroom. He couldn't deny it— the man lying in that bed was clearly fading and far from invincible. Cotton recalls a look of sadness in his father's soulful eyes.

After what seemed to be a small eternity, but was no longer than about an hour, there were still no signs of the doctor. This time, with more urgency, Lottie sent Cotton off, who again ran as fast as his legs would take him down the two more miles of dirt road back to Five Points. This time, he didn't arrive as a polite and agreeable child. In that instant, with the forcefulness of a young man far beyond his years, Cotton's determination seemed to move Dr. Deck to finally drop what he was doing, pack up his black bag, and make the trek to attend to Horace Young. "My heart was pounding so wildly, I swear Dr. Deck could hear the blood pumping through my veins," remembers Cotton, who did not leave the office until certain that the doctor was indeed on his way. Adrenaline fueled him to finish the eight-mile marathon on that fateful day.

Silence and fear pervaded the atmosphere at the Young homestead. When the doctor finally arrived and was ushered to Horace's bedside, the anticipation was palpable, for the family's future hung in the balance of Dr. Deck's pronouncement.

Before too long, he emerged to a line of anxious faces, and announced, "It's just a case of indigestion. Your father will be fine and fit for work in the morning." Relief rippled through the house and some semblance of normalcy returned. Everything would be okay after all. Nine children laid their heads on their pillows that night and slept without a care, as should be the privilege of the young. No one thought to question the doctor's diagnosis, because back then this simply wasn't done. However, Cotton awoke from his little boy dreams only to discover a real-life nightmare.

From the contorted mix of shock and sorrow on his mother's face, Cotton knew there was trouble. For any child, it was trouble of the worst kind. Horace Young, at age 40, had died in his sleep. Cotton glanced towards the bedroom where he just saw his dad last night. *How could it be?* Surely his father would walk out at any moment and ask when breakfast would be ready. Cotton's thoughts raced. He thought about the last words exchanged between him and his father, the last time his father was angry with him and the last time he was proud of him. *Was he ever proud of me?* The official ruling on the death certificate was indigestion. It wouldn't be until many years later that Cotton realized his father had died, far too young, of a massive heart attack.

In the blink of an eye the Young family had changed forever. No longer carefree, the sense of safety and security that always "just was," now was inexplicably gone. The custom of keeping the coffin in the household parlor for several days after a loved one's death further magnified the family's grief. There was no escaping the grim reality of this great loss.

And then there was Lottie. Her husband was such a dominant presence, a man's man from whom she drew strength. She may have been the heart of the home, but Horace was the backbone and breadwinner.

To make matters worse, hard times had simultaneously fallen on the entire country. The American dream was in the process of becoming a nightmare as the prosperity of the Roaring Twenties began to give way on "Black Tuesday," October 29, 1929—the day the stock market crashed, sending shock waves all through the United States and throughout the industrialized Western world. Panic and unemployment rose sharply. The extremes of wealth and poverty, of power and impotence, began to intensify.

If the odds were stacked against survival in a two-parent household, what would become of this single mother and her family of 11? Though Lottie attempted to mask her fears, the unspoken question was, "How will we possibly make ends meet?" During a time when people began roaming the country in search of food, work and shelter, her fears were certainly justified. "Everyone was restless," Cotton remembers, "trying to find work, trying to feed their families. Men were in the streets, shining shoes, peddling newspapers or selling apples...doing anything they could." Little did the young boy know that it would take a dozen years and the eve of war to put the economy back together once again. What had been known as the land of opportunity was instead becoming the land of desperation.

Cotton's older brother was honorably discharged and returned home from the Navy to help contribute to the family finances. Still, Cotton inherently knew his childhood was over and immediately applied for what was called "continuation school." In hardship cases, certain students were allowed to attend school one day a week for two years, working the rest of the week to help support their families. It was the perfect—and only—tonic to assuage Cotton's grief and meet the needs of the Young household. He never thought of his actions in terms of sacrifice or heroism. When asked about his self-sacrificial act today, Cotton dismisses it, and with the clear vision of age looking back to youth says, "I just did what I had to do."

The sense of duty and honor instilled in Cotton by Horace was the inheritance left to him by his father. Cotton seemed to learn at a young age that if he couldn't avoid adversity, he would find a way to overcome it—to create meaning out of it. With the same fervor that propelled him down that dirt road to seek help, Cotton's determination to keep the family afloat actually set him on course to discover his destiny.

His misfortune would turn into a lifelong love affair. And Cotton was to the fairway born.

Cotton Young (center)
holding the pin for his player.

The First Tee

IT IS SAID TO BE IN THE LAND of kilts and bagpipes that privileged gentlemen playing the game of golf first hired laborers on a regular basis to carry clubs for them. These *cawdys* (a term used to describe traveling water carriers and messengers in 18th-century Scotland) scratched out a living looping and were the forerunner of today's caddies.

When golf arrived on America's shores from the windswept Scottish coast just before the 20th century and the game took off in popularity, demand necessitated that each country club establish a caddie pool, which was modeled after the European system. A caddie master would assign caddies to players and was responsible to watch over financial and discipline matters.

The best hope of early caddies was that they were matched with players whose body types were comparable to their own so that they could "inherit" hand me downs. Clothing was much harder to come by in the days before department stores and shopping malls dotted the American landscape.

As an example of the hedonistic excess of the Roaring Twenties, some wealthy players would actually hire two caddies—one to carry the bags and one to cover himself in jelly in order to attract flies away from the golfers. (Honest, this is a true story!) They were known as "jam boys." Caddies have come a long way since their jam boy days. Today, according to Cotton, a veteran looper is responsible to:

- Know the rules
- Clean and maintain the equipment
- Fix the divots
- Rake the sand traps
- Find and mark a player's ball
- Determine and calculate accurate yardages to various key points on the course
- Have a detailed understanding of the course layout and architecture
- Know from which direction the prevailing winds are most likely to blow

- Understand basic golf strategies most suited to the player and the course
- Be familiar with the player's strengths and weaknesses
- Be familiar with the unique characteristics of each green, including slope, speed rating, pin placement and grain
- Give reliable advice on club selection and shot execution
- Keep track of the players' scores
- Remain excited, despite the game's score
- Be able to inspire confidence
- Be consistent
- Have a sense of humor
- Be a voice of reason and calmness
- Provide emotional support during times of competitive pressure.

This extensive list also reveals that looping is an appealing profession for those who wish to stay healthy. Those who might consider becoming caddies should know that great levels of endurance are necessary. Toting 30-50 pounds of golf equipment over a rolling 7,000-yard course will certainly keep you trim and fit—but blisters, muscle cramps and pulls, backaches, and just plain exhaustion can await the green caddie.

The stereotypical caddie in the early 20th century may have been impoverished, hard-drinking, bawdy, rough hewn, and more than slightly acquainted with a sailor's salty vocabulary. However, if you were a Saucon Valley Country Club looper, you were generally a good-natured, gentlemanly rogue who could play a fair game of golf and walk just about anyone into the ground. (This despite a propensity to smoke or chew tobacco, drink too much coffee and enjoy more than your fair share of beer.)

Today Cotton can't quite recall where he falls in the succession of his 12 siblings, but though almost eight decades have passed, the memory of his first day at the Saucon Valley Country Club is as vivid as ever.

The 13-year-old Cotton arrived at Saucon about 8 a.m. after walking to Five Points from his home, then hitchhiking the 10 or so miles to the club gates. Cotton says, "Finding a ride wasn't easy in 1929 because there were so few people who owned cars." Cotton watched the early morning fog evaporate in wisps sweeping the dew from greens that looked like billiard tables. He was met by the caddie master, who wasted no time giving Cotton his first assignment. If he could accomplish it, he would be rewarded with a quarter, right on the spot. Cotton and two of the older caddies made their way down to the creek at the ninth hole.

Hanging from a tree over the water was a looped rope; all Cotton had to do for his reward was jump out a few feet and catch it. He cavalierly sized up the task and determined, "This will be the easiest 25 cents I'll ever earn." Cotton confidently launched out, only to have the rope pulled up and out of his reach. Following his ungraceful spill into the waist-deep water, he realized there was another caddie in the tree working in cahoots with the caddie master. This was Cotton's initiation into the caddie "pool." He was sworn to secrecy not to warn rookie caddies of the dangers that lurked at the ninth hole.

Youngsters were the mainstay of the caddie pool, mainly because they were willing to carry a member's clubs for 20 cents an hour. One of the perks was that all caddies could play the course for free every Monday morning. Cotton enthusiastically states, "I can't think of a better way for a kid to learn the game than to play one round and then caddie a second. Combine a decent pay check with an occasional swing here and there, and you may turn kids away from TV and video games for a little while." Plus, on a practical level, a serious interest in golf is just bound to keep kids out of trouble. "Golf takes time," says Cotton. "You're not going to be out running the streets if you really want to become good at golf." Looping was known to be a wholesome and enriching exploit for adolescents. Caddies could earn competitive wages and fall in love with a game that holds integrity and honesty as its core values. For some, caddying provided the opportunity to meet businessmen who would later offer them a job.

Today the Saucon Valley Country Club has a caddie committee with a chairman. New caddies are required to attend three 2½ hour sessions of caddie training where they learn a range of skills including studying the yardages and greens and learning the time-honored rules of golf. Rookie caddies are limited to one bag and are assigned to an honor caddie for on-the-greens training. Every looper has a rating card with one of three classifications: novice, regular and honor caddie. Each is paid commensurate with experience and a looper's tip is dependent on the quality of service given. After each round, players have the opportunity to appraise each caddie on the backside of the rating card.

Back in the early days, learning to caddie was truly "on the bag" training. Cotton literally got thrown into the fire without the luxury of a rookie learning curve. Mr. Walter Bourlier, Cotton's very first player

said, "Come on caddie, we're going up to No. 10."
On the way, Cotton took time to savor the splendor
of the scene. Coming from sparse and somewhat drab
living conditions, he was awed by the beauty of the
course, even with 20 pounds of equipment tugging
against his virgin shoulder. It was love at first sight
for Cotton, who seemed to have a magical connection
with the greens.

After their arrival on the 10th tee, Mr. Bourlier
said, "Here are two balls; one's Jack and one's Jill. Pick
one." Not realizing the implications of his indecision,
Cotton picked both. Being a good sport, Mr. Bourlier
played not one, but two balls for nine holes. Cotton
exclaims, "I watched him hit his first drive off the
tee, a drive that hit the heart of the fairway, and I
was hooked." He was hooked on the people, hooked
on the daily dose of nature, the quiet sanctuary filled
with trees, rolling hills, curving fairways, and the
greenest grass ever seen. For Cotton, looping was like
a walk in the park, a climb up a hill and a stroll along
a creek—even if he carried a bag that was nearly his
height, and on hills where his shoulder couldn't go
high enough, had to be lifted by the handle to keep it
from dragging on the ground.

That first day he caddied for an hour and a half
and earned 30 cents. Beaming with pride, Cotton

couldn't wait to rush his first pay home to his mother. "In the days when 30 cents bought a loaf of bread and six cans of baked beans," Cotton says, "I made enough to feed the whole family dinner that night."

Common tips in those days were apples, pennies and sometimes cookies. A woman once tipped Cotton two gingersnaps. In 2002, after hearing about Cotton's two-gingersnap tip, a female golfer treated him to two pounds of the cookies. To this day, Cotton receives holiday gift baskets filled with homemade treats from his not-so-secret female admirers.

In his dedication to caring for his family, Cotton became smitten with the game and was eager to pick up as many loops as he possibly could. He would regularly caddie 18 holes, and 36 holes when available, teeing up when the sun was barely peeking out through the golf course's early morning mist. He sometimes continued until the sunset cast long, graceful shadows over the eighteenth racing the darkness to finish the back nine when the natural light was at its richest and the colors of nature took on their most brilliant hues. This conscientious caddie never missed a day on the greens except for once a week attendance at continuance school, and when he was forced to further supplement his family's income by cleaning bobbins in a local silk mill. All the while,

Cotton longed for the fresh air of the fairways.

As he learned the ropes of golf he began to contribute to the game, though not on a grand scale. Saucon members began to recognize Cotton's ability to add something special to their experience. He embraced the core values of golf, including courtesy, respect, discipline, and honor. The simple act of picking up a piece of trash that found a place on the course was his subtle way of making a difference. Fixing divots and repairing ball marks on the green were tasks he considered of premium importance.

As time passed, he began to develop a sense of connectedness to golf—to the course, the players, and to the heritage of the game. Out of respect for the game and his players, Cotton valued decorum and tradition, and demonstrated a scrupulous but not prudish regard for the rules of golf. When Cotton went to sleep at night, he didn't count sheep—he counted birdies.

In any player-caddie relationship, the player sets the tone. Ultimately, the player decides if there will be chit-chat between shots, or if there will be discussions about which club to hit or what line to take. In the end, the player determines if the caddie's role will be that of a servant or an advisor—or something in between. One of the secrets to being a good caddie is to have the ability to read players' moods. Knowing when to laugh or lament, speak or remain silent, get involved or look the other way is essential. A shadowy separation most likely existed between caddies and members, but if so, Cotton never makes mention of it.

His motto has always been, "Never give advice unless asked. Don't play the player's game for them, but be ready to contribute if called upon." Cotton began putting himself in the player's shoes and would pretend that *he* was hitting the shots; thinking about what *he* would do. That way he stayed ready should his opinion be requested.

Caddies must also become familiar with a player's personality and game. Cotton learned to "club" players by feel and sight, not by using a yard book. Cotton explains, "I learned all of my golfers' yardages and how far they tended to hit each club under ideal circumstances." Caddies adept at club selection quickly gained golfers' favor and players started to show faith in Cotton. He felt a certain satisfaction when he would positively influence a shot by choosing the right club for the job. Cotton played a role, albeit a tiny one, in helping members improve their games.

In time, the tow-headed boy looper became a bona fide caddie. No longer just a bag-toter,

Cotton embraced the extra responsibility and eventually found himself among the caddie elite. Establishing seniority among the caddies, he became one of the top five among the 300 or so in the caddie pool.

After looping for 10 years, Cotton won first honors (and a cash prize) for meritorious caddie service. This award was based on best all around service, courtesy, and best reporting record. To this day, he has the newspaper clipping dated Saturday, October 28, 1939, featuring his photo with Saucon's then-president, J. M. Sylvester.

Cotton's popularity had risen to such heights by the late 1950s that he was chosen to appear in the booklet, "Responsibilities of a Golfer," published by the Saucon Valley Country Club. This dapper caddie can be seen in several photos demonstrating the proper care and treatment of the greens with Saucon's then-golf professional, Ralph Hutchison. Many surmise that Cotton's striking good looks were among the contributing factors in being chosen for this honor.

To Cotton, the combination of great men and a great game was part of the allure of his profession. Drawn in by the caliber of these men, this dedicated looper found a profitable way to stay close to the game and the people he loved. But Cotton's life was not made wholly complete on the greens. The missing element was yet to come—not on the fairways, but on a hilltop.

Cotton and Ralph Hutchison, SVCC golf professional for 39 years, as they appeared in the booklet, "Responsibilities of a Golfer"

Love Off the Links

COTTON WAS NO LONGER A BOY. With his striking blonde hair, suspenders, white buck shoes, and baby blue tie, he cut quite a fashionable figure. His charm and gentle ways, the strong arms of a caddie and the sparkle in his eye ensured that he had no shortage of female admirers. Seeing photos of Cotton as a young man, many exclaim, "He looks like a young Robert Redford!" though Cotton preceded the movie star by at least two decades. Many girls chased him—but only one ultimately caught his eye.

As the mercury plummeted in late December, sledding was Cotton's recreational pastime of choice. He remembers many a wintry day spent sledding down snow-covered hills, though none stands out as prominently as one day in 1936. "When the snow came, our street was a gathering spot for kids of all ages out sledding. My family lived at the top of the hill, so our first trip down was free," Cotton recalls with a chuckle.

Few families could afford the solid hardwood sleds with hand-cut finger holes of the day (plastics had not been invented as yet), so neighborhood kids took turns sharing a few sleds to race up and down Benner Avenue. While impatiently waiting for a turn, Cotton noticed a lovely dark-eyed girl with a pretty face and a figure to match. He sauntered over and, while making small talk, discovered that this particular girl was one of the Breidingers—a family that lived in a home at the halfway point on Benner Avenue. Cotton mustered up the nerve to ask Florence if she'd like to sled with him, to which she demurely smiled and replied, "Perhaps I will."

From that day Cotton and Florence dated each other exclusively. Like all kids of their generation, the young couple loved big bands and went dancing together as often as they could. "We also went roller skating on weeknights, but our big date of the week was a motion picture at the movie house in Bethlehem," Cotton says animatedly. In 1936, this young suitor spent a dollar to escort his girl to the movies. "A far cry from the 15 cents I spent as a kid that included admission to see a silent movie, a hot dog and a free orange soda." (For those who can't imagine seeing a movie without popcorn, this treat didn't become standard movie fare until the 1940s.) "Even at those rates," Cotton says, "certain boys were known to slip in without paying. If the manager ever caught them, he would hit them with a cane." Back then, caning was an acceptable form of public discipline.

In 1936, the same year FDR delivered his second inaugural address with the poignant line, "I see one-third of a nation ill-housed, ill-clad, ill-nourished," Americans were flocking to the movies as a means of escape from the harsh reality of every day life. Moviegoers were astonished at the innovation of Greta Garbo's debut "talkie" film, when a record was played for sound while the reel was shown. Later, movie houses adapted arc-lamp projectors to provide audio. These cinematic and technological developments for Cotton's generation are akin to the captivating special effects of a 21st century movie. "Seeing and hearing a movie—at the same time— was a real thrill!" Cotton exclaims. For Cotton and Florence and most Americans, still in the midst of the Depression, the movies represented a glimpse of a future full of promise instead of a reflection of the grim past.

As is the case with young love, Cotton and Florence would extend their Friday night dates as long as possible. As often as Cotton's caddie wages would allow, they would stop and linger on the way home for ice cream floats at the local drugstore. "Florence wasn't like any girl I had ever met. She was my first and only love," says Cotton, his voice awash with nostalgia and emotion. Truly a love match, nobody had to bring them together or promote their union—they were both entirely smitten. A whirlwind romance between the dashing, 21-year-old caddie and the adoring, 19-year-old beauty ended Cotton's days of bachelorhood. They married in a civil ceremony on June 3, 1937, less than six months after that first sled ride.

Once the Young and Breidinger families merged, there was never a dull moment. This was a large and humorous family, which is evidenced by the colorful nicknames of the brothers and sisters: Fat, Cheetah, Baulky, Yidi, Wip, Pinky and Goc were just a few! With Ross known as Cotton and Florence known as "Fats" (by the way, she was given that moniker when she was poker-thin) and sometimes "Flossy," they both fit right in. How they distinguished "Fat" from "Fats" is still a mystery.

Following their simple wedding, Cotton and his new bride moved into their first home on Benner Avenue. Early in their marriage they would live in three different houses all on—you guessed it—Benner Avenue.

It wasn't long before the stork flew in with a baby girl who Cotton and Flossy named Dolores Mae. She would grow up in that small town and later give birth to her own five children in St. Luke's Hospital—the same hospital where she was born. Her sister Pat wouldn't come along for another 14 years and youngest sibling, Barbara, four years after that. A pixie of a little girl with her father's blonde hair and big, summer-blue eyes, Dolores was known to be precocious, which can be typical of a first child. It was her quick thinking as a nine-year-old that once bungled an attempted burglary. On the Young family's first night at another new home on Benner Avenue, Dolores was suddenly awakened from sleep by someone entering the front door. Not missing a beat, she yelled out, "Dad, get your gun!" which was enough to send the intruder fleeing right back out the way he came. Unbeknownst to the uninvited guest, Cotton didn't even own a gun. Though unharmed, the family was a bit spooked after the experience, so the three of them fled to Cotton's mother's home that night, never again to return to that residence (except to pack).

The age gap between Dolores and her sisters gave her a certain authority in the home. Fourteen years younger, Pat was the flower girl in Dolores' wedding and Barbara grew up more like her daughter than her sister. It was 16-year-old Dolores who was the first to drive in the Young family, and she was the one to finally teach her father to drive at age 40. Florence never did learn, which wasn't all that unusual in the 1950s.

Noting the virtues of Cotton's life is an easy task, but not so with his flaws. In all the years his daughters grew up under his roof they unanimously agree: "We never knew Dad to raise his voice or to utter a mean word." That is quite a legacy, especially for a lone male in a household of females.

Cotton's personal price for making ends meet was that his three daughters grew to womanhood seemingly unnoticed. For 40 years he not only caddied, but also worked full-time at Bethlehem Steel. In what seemed like the blink of an eye, his little girls had little girls of their own—and they, too had little girls who themselves were no longer children.

Though Cotton wasn't stern like his father and never raised a hand to his daughters, he was undemonstrative and didn't readily share his feelings with his children. Cotton's way of expressing his love was by providing. Florence inherently understood this and never made an issue of the long hours away from home, even if that meant his occasional absence on holidays. She and the children greatly benefited from all of Cotton's looping labors, and Florence never had to worry about finances. From the start of their marriage Cotton says, "I gave my wife five dollars a week "mad" money to spend however she wanted." Over the years Florence's share grew to 50 percent of her husband's caddie coffer. Each time he trekked to the golf course, he was, in his way, loving her and loving their daughters.

Cotton's Saucon Valley life and family life were of two distinctly separate worlds, and it never occurred to Cotton or Florence to bring the two together. Florence never visited the club, never saw the caddie shack and never met Cotton's players. It wasn't until 2004 that the first of Cotton's family, his youngest daughter Barbara, visited Saucon for a grand tour of the grounds. "Dad was driving me all around with his left leg casually hanging over the side of the golf cart," Barbara exclaims. "It was one of the best experiences I ever shared with my father." If Cotton was preoccupied with work while his children grew up, he made up for the loss with his grandchildren. Each summer they visited their grandparents' home—a bed and breakfast of sorts where Nana (as Florence was called by her grandchildren) would prepare a made-to-order breakfast every morning. Even if one wanted pancakes with scrapple (a Pennsylvania Dutch favorite) and another wanted eggs, home fries and fried ring bologna (another Pennsylvania Dutch favorite), it was no problem at the Young B & B.

Florence was pretty sassy, never hesitating to offer a shot glass of beer to the grandkids during games of Yahtzee, Scrabble, or Gin Rummy (much to their parent's chagrin). She abandoned herself to the role of a hairdresser's client as her granddaughters endlessly brushed and set her hair with rollers and rubbed Jergens lotion into her hands—a child's mock version of a manicure. Fresh smelling laundry is nostalgic aromatherapy that brings back memories of the sheets Nana hung outside on the clothesline before lovingly making the beds.

Pop-Pop, as Cotton was called by his grandchildren, would be long gone to the country club by the time the little guests woke up, but when he returned home after his customary 18 holes, he came bearing all kinds of treats. Cotton, who did all the grocery shopping for the household, would buy the grandkids absolutely anything they desired. On the top ten list was Tang: "After all, the astronauts are drinking it." Cotton would exclaim. Pennsylvania Dutch delicacies like Gibble's chips, ring and Lebanon bologna, Cooper cheese, donuts, and of course, all the Popsicles and ice cream they could eat were highlights of a stay at Nana's and Pop-Pop's.

Florence was known for baking the best homemade pies, like her no-spice pumpkin, which still remains a family favorite that few in the world have ever heard of or tried. Today granddaughter Beth continues her grandmother's culinary tradition of expert pie-making. Florence baked rhubarb and sour cherry custard, apple and lemon meringue pies, and holiday memories are filled with baking and eating her delectable kiffles, (granddaughter Kari makes her grandmother's kiffles annually at Christmas time in her honor), jam-filled "kisses" (daughter Barbara continues this holiday tradition) and cut-out sugar cookies. Though Florence's own decorated baked goods were known to be both beautiful and delicious, she feigned to love the way the girls decorated their reindeer, stars and Christmas trees, even if they were somewhat of a mess according to the Betty Crocker standards of the day. Florence's culinary repertoire was not limited only to sweets. She also received rave reviews for her savory chicken potpie, which her family still views as the epitome of comfort food.

Most find it surprising to hear of a caddie who cooks and bakes. But then, Cotton's not your average caddie. He is famed for his chili con carne and molasses crumb and funnel cakes.

Cotton regularly entertained the kids with masterful drawings of bunny rabbits and by walking across the room on his hands, showcasing brawny forearms reminiscent of Popeye. Miniature golf was a favorite outing, because Cotton could relish his trifecta of favorite roles—caddie, golfer and grandfather. As you can imagine, he regularly wowed everyone with his string of holes-in-one.

Betraying the era they were from, Cotton and Florence called the toilet a "hopper." This was carried over from the contraption in the first "water closets", which were conical-shaped hoppers set in lead traps. Their car? It was known as the "sheeny" (an abbreviation from the days when cars were called machines), and it was a beauty. In the sheeny, which was a winged-back, blue and cream metallic Mercury with big, round lights and a back window that went completely down, they would make trips down bumpy Saucon Valley Road, known by the children as "Ticklebelly Road," which rivaled the rides at nearby

Dorney Park, the children's favorite Allentown attraction.

A regular destination in the sheeny on Ticklebelly Road was an ice cold, fresh spring bubbling from the rocks at the side of the road. There they filled containers with gallons of water that Cotton touted as the Fountain of Youth. Of course, his grandchildren believed him. They believed everything Pop-Pop said. Some of those magic waters must have splashed on Cotton.

Though the Young family did eventually move from Benner Avenue, they have never lived any other place than Bethlehem. In fact, Cotton's phone number has remained the same for over 50 years! Bethlehem, a quaint and charming town known as "The Christmas City" began as a Moravian settlement. The Moravians were responsible for naming their village Bethlehem on Christmas Eve 1741 after the historic city of Christ's birth. Later it was famous for being at the crossroads of the Industrial Revolution when steel would reign for a hundred years. Today you can ride in a horse-drawn carriage through Bethlehem's historic district. There you will find the Moravian Book Shop—the oldest, continuously running bookstore in the United States—founded in 1745 by the Moravian Church. One popular destination and a favorite of Cotton's grandchildren during the holiday season is the Community Putz (pronounced like the word puts) at the Central Moravian Church. Each year, this historic church displays the nativity story through narration, lights and an elaborate miniature landscape. Just like the star that led wise men to the ancient city of Bethlehem, the Bethlehem Star still shines brightly up on South Mountain. The 91-foot-high electric star was installed in 1937 and became a sign of hope to a Depression-torn region.

The star remained dark after the Japanese bombing of Pearl Harbor in Hawaii on December 7, 1941, forcing America into war. Bethlehem Steel responded to President Roosevelt's challenge that the United States become "the great arsenal of democracy." Planes, tanks, guns and ships were built with unprecedented speed to defeat the nation's enemies. This made the city a likely military target. So the star, which could be seen for miles when lit at night, had to be blacked out for the duration of the war. This symbol of "peace on earth and good will towards men" was fittingly re-lit after four years by a mother whose son went missing in action. Today, not only is the Bethlehem Star lit all year long, but also miniature versions can be found lighting up thousands of homes all throughout the

Christmas City.

Despite the many charms of this unique hometown, nothing rivals Cotton's favorite Bethlehem destination. Bethlehem Steel may have put Bethlehem, Pennsylvania on America's industrial map, but on the golf landscape, Bethlehem is best known for forging one of the finest country clubs in the nation—Cotton's second home, the Saucon Valley Country Club.

The 21-year-old Cotton

The lifelong looper in his role as "father of the bride"
pictured with his oldest daughter Dolores, his wife,
Florence, and youngest daughter, Barbara

Peter O'Krepki

Cotton's indelible mark can be found in the blond tuft
capping the head of great-grandson, Bobby Boggs, Jr.

Grandeur in the Grass

GOLF IS UNIQUELY DISTINGUISHED by its playing field. While stadiums have their allure, many rate the rich beauty of the golf course as the most varied and interesting arena in sports. Equal parts beauty and challenge, the Saucon Valley Country Club stands out in the golf world for having not one, not two, but three pristinely maintained, Top-100, championship courses. Few clubs anywhere in the world offer three courses of such caliber under the big blue sky. People from all corners of the globe and from all walks of life have marveled at the beauty and conditioning of Saucon's courses. In fact, in 1997, the nation's leading course-ranking panel rated Saucon's courses as numbers four, seven and eight in Pennsylvania.

This is notable in a state where the competition includes Merion, Oakmont and an abundance of courses designed by famed architects William Flynn, Donald Ross, and A.W. Tillinghast.

Saucon's historic "Old Course" dates back to 1922 and lies nestled in the Lehigh Valley about 45 miles north of Philadelphia. It was designed by the renowned English-born designer Herbert Strong. The land was once designated for meadows and fields of corn, wheat and clover, which explains Saucon's relaxed pastoral setting. Strong was famous for designing courses like the Engineers' Club at Roslyn, New York, the Canterbury Golf Club near Cleveland, Ohio, and the Ponte Vedra Club in Florida, home to one of golf's first island greens. His payment? The handsome sum of $125 a day, a sizable paycheck at the time, plus expenses for his efforts while working on the Saucon Valley course.

The Old Course, considered the Club's classic, features rolling hills and is framed by mature, majestic trees. Many duffers describe the stately oaks, maples and willows that line the course as "big trees with gravitational pull," referring to their seeming propensity to magnetically attract golf balls. Legend has it that strong men have crumbled before the subtle, treacherous undulations of the Old Course greens.

Requiring mastery of every shot, even the most accurate drivers are challenged when faced with the narrow landing areas so stingily offered by the fickle lady. "Some players swear the greens shrink while they're looking at them," Cotton chuckles. Saucon's proud Old Course seems to present every challenge offered by the game, including every imaginable hazard as well as reward. "Not many can play 18 holes without finding a tree, a bunker or a creek," Cotton says respectfully of the Old Course. The demands are great, the challenge is inspiring and the experience downright satisfying.

This course was chosen for use by the United States Golf Association's (USGA) 1951 U.S. Amateur Championship, the 1983 U.S. Junior Championship, the 1987 U.S. Senior Amateur Championship, and the 1992 and 2000 U.S. Senior Open tournaments. In Ralph Grayson Schwarz's book, *Saucon Valley Country Club—An American Legacy 1920-2000*, USGA Deputy Director Michael Butz says:

> In 20 years of conducting USGA championships, I have had the distinct privilege of visiting a large number of golf clubs, and very simply, Saucon Valley Country Club has the most unique combination of golf, sports and recreation facilities in the United States in perhaps the most peaceful and relaxed setting. It provides an enjoyable experience whether you are a beginner golfer, nature lover, or golfer of the highest order.

Though any of the approximately 17,000 country clubs throughout the United States would covet hosting even *one* national championship, Saucon has hosted five. Through all of these USGA events, the club has attained enduring national status. "Saucon will host its sixth USGA championship—the U.S. Women's Open—in 2009," Cotton says, swelling with pride. That number could be even higher, but the club has limited such hosting engagements by choice.

The Grace Course is the namesake of a man who never held a formal position at Saucon, but was known as the club founder and patriarch, Eugene Gifford Grace. Completed in 1957, the course—long and challenging with massive bunkers—has been named to *Golf Digest's* "Top 100 Golf Courses" ever since rankings were first recorded in 1966. The Grace Course differs from the Old Course in the open character of its terrain. Director of Golf Gene Mattare says, "The Grace Course is a long, demanding course that forces the golfer to use virtually every club in the bag." It circles the Old Course with a classic parkland layout. The treacherous Saucon Creek guards the greens with numerous water hazards as it serpentines through the course, and crosses over the 10th hole twice. It's been said that brave men have stood on the back tees of the Grace course and quivered. But it's not all danger, toils and snares. "When temperatures dip low enough for long enough," Cotton says, "The pond located on the 8th hole is sometimes used as an ice skating rink."

Some consider the club's third course, Weyhill, which opened in 1968, to be the most picturesque. Laid out over what had once been a dairy farm named Weyhill Farms, each hole is a photo opportunity of magnificent views and dramatic changes in elevation. Reflecting another era, Weyhill features old limekilns, slate-roofed barns and an abandoned quarry. The quarry, located on a par-3 hole, drops 60 feet straight down. According to Cotton, in addition to wildflowers and lush greenery adorning the quarry walls, "a red fox calls it home."

It would not be unusual to spot many varieties of wildlife while visiting the 850-acre country club. Wild turkeys, deer, bobcats, and even the occasional bear or coyote provide the authentic backdrop to the Saucon Valley experience, with the meandering Saucon Creek intertwined throughout all three of its grand courses.

One story that speaks to the mingling of nature with the game of golf is when in 1956, George Wiehl, a golfer in St. Joseph, Missouri, stepped up to the tee and whacked a long drive down the fairway. He watched with satisfaction until it came to a sudden halt. A woodpecker, flying the other way, had impaled the ball on its beak!* This unbelievable story gives new meaning to the phrase, "He shot a birdie."

Ask members to name their favorite courses and, unfailingly, their responses are evenly split. To Cotton, however, none compare to his beloved Old Course. After all, this is where he got his first start on the bag. His personal history is intertwined with the history of the Old Course.

Today, Cotton makes his way through the Old Course with intimate familiarity, his left leg hanging ever so casually over the side of his cart. Each hole has a story that is bound in his memory and is part of the fabric of his life. To him, each hole on the course is akin to an unforgettable person who grows more interesting with each visit.

Of the 18th named Dogleg, Cotton boasts, "Larry Laoretti made a great shot—a 20 foot uphill chip with a 5-iron—to win the U.S. Senior Open back in '92." Of the 10th called Buttonwood, he says, "This is a birdie hole. Club founder Eugene Grace added the bunkers on the left almost over night to make the hole harder during the 1951 U.S. Amateurs." Of the 4th, named Willows, Cotton says, "Jerry Barber

*Astonishing but True Golf Facts, Allan Zullo.

[for whom Cotton caddied in the 1992 U.S. Senior Open] said he hated this hole. It's long, and you have to be sure to clear the trees on the left."

"There used to be a two-seater outhouse about a hundred yards from the third tee inside the long, out-of-bounds fence that runs down to the creek. It sure came as a welcome relief to both golfers and caddies," Cotton chuckles.

With so many years at Saucon, Cotton's knowledge of the greens is encyclopedic. He knows every blade of grass on the Old Course, his intuition formed by years of experience and careful observation. "Measuring distance is only a part of it," Cotton says. "There are so many other things to consider: the strength and direction of wind, the firmness of the ground, the shape of the green and the shape of the shot."

It came as no surprise when, in preparation for the 2000 U.S. Senior Open hosted by Saucon, Cotton was asked to offer his hole-by-hole insights in the June 28, 2000 edition of Allentown's leading newspaper, *The Morning Call.* This special 24-page, full-color newspaper insert featured Cotton on almost every page. His photo accompanied the heading: "Cotton says" followed by his sage advice for mastering each hole. "Long hitters can get home with a driver and a wedge. But if the pin is behind the right trap, it's almost an impossible putt," Cotton says of the 8th called Evergreens. Of the 17th named Turtle, Cotton says, "This is the toughest green to read on the course. Putts break the opposite of how they look, and it's always fast."

Before rakes were invented to prepare bunkers (caddies formerly used golf clubs to smooth the disrupted sand), Cotton says, "It took a heck of a lot more effort back then." At a time when distance markers were non-existent, Cotton knew every distance—not with a yardage book, but with his eyes. Part of the seen-it-all, done-it-all caddie brigade, Cotton possessed the kind of knowledge that made him indispensable when the U.S. Amateur Championship and the Old Course met in 1951.

Only on a few occasions in his 77 years of looping did a golf ball hit Cotton—no small achievement, considering that he regularly made himself a human target in order to give his players a line, charging the members to shoot the ball over his head while teeing off on the 3rd hole of the Old Course. When golfers expressed concerns for his safety, Cotton replied, "I've never been hit yet, but the first one who does gets a box of golf balls." It has been 77 years and Cotton has never given away a single ball.

During the 1951 U.S. Amateur Championship,

players were still responsible to supply their own balls for practice shots. Cotton was struck while picking up his player's shag balls. He was ducking and dodging the vexatious dimpled spheres dropping all around him like hailstones when from out of nowhere contestant Bobby Knowles shot a drive blast that sliced straight toward Cotton with the precise aim of a sniper. The moving ball, filled with peril, hit him directly in the back, leaving him with a quickly swelling, purple welt. Undeterred, he continued on with the job at hand.

At the 1951 Amateurs, Cotton caddied for Dale Morey, winner of both the North and South Amateurs. "I caddied for Morey for three rounds, and he was never down until the very end. He beat two players and was tied with Harold Paddock, Jr. on the 18th. Then, we watched in amazement as Paddock sunk a 51-foot putt to beat Morey on the 20th." Those who have experienced the "so close and yet so far" aspect of tournament play well know there is a reason why golf is a *four-letter* word.

A caddie must maintain a precise but shifting balance between involvement and invisibility. Cotton was always one to share in his player's highs as well as commiserate with the lows. He may not have hit a single shot, but his local knowledge of the links was integral to every play that Morey made. By the end of the tournament these qualities made such an impression on Morey that he wrote a letter to the Saucon Valley Country Club Board of Governors expressing his appreciation for Cotton's caddie prowess.

The 1951 U.S. Amateur marked Cotton's last tournament that still included the *stymie* in its rules of play. A stymie occurred when a player's golf ball obstructed the line between the opponent's ball and the hole. When prevented from reaching the hole directly, you were said to be "stymied." The player was then required to hit over or around the ball.

No specific rule introduced stymie play into golf. It resulted from the cardinal law of golf that you never picked up your ball until you have holed out. Originally, stymie situations were accidental occurrences, but some golfers figured out the competitive advantage of intentionally stymieing their opponent's ball, a strategy also used effectively in billiards.

In 1951, when the USGA and the Royal & Ancient Golf Club of St. Andrews agreed to consolidate the rules on both sides of "the pond" for a 1952 joint edition of the Rules of Golf, the Brits insisted upon maintaining the hard-set rule of not picking up a ball on the green. The Americans lobbied for a rule permitting the marking and picking up of a ball, mainly because stymies slowed play. You know the outcome, and when the rules became effective in 1952, the stymie was no more. Some golfers celebrated this change in rules heartily as one less complication in their quest to save par while others mourned the loss of their arguably unfair advantage.

Just as the game of golf has changed, Saucon has gone through an evolution of its own. Today it is hard to believe that this charming acreage was once a dusty cornfield. Saucon Valley now boasts a recreation complex that spreads out over nearly 850 acres. Though golf may be the singular activity that drives the community, in addition to 60 holes of golf including a six-hole junior course, there are more than a dozen tennis courts, squash courts and platform tennis. Just beyond the classic Georgian red brick clubhouse with its four white anchoring pillars is a grassy slope that leads to a swimming pool complex comprised of two children's pools, a lap pool and finally, an Olympic-size pool. Cotton is an accomplished swimmer and enjoyed a dip now and then when the pool was open to loopers during caddie tourneys and picnics. He could be found effortlessly floating on his back with his eyes closed for such long periods of time that others wondered if he could actually be napping. Their curiosity was satisfied when Cotton would suddenly break out whistling a tune.

It comes as no surprise that Saucon's lush bentgrass tees and carpet-like fairways are anything but "par for the course." The playing surfaces are nearly flawless and even the dense stand of bluegrass and fescue-mixed rough looks beautiful—that is, until your ball sails merrily into it.

No one ever had to remind Cotton to stop and smell the scent of freshly mown grass. He was satisfied to live in and enjoy the moment. For Cotton, connecting with players, working outside, experiencing the colors and sounds of nature while giving away the talents he possessed in service to others awakened his senses and revitalized his soul daily.

There is one more location nestled on the grounds of the famed Saucon Valley Country Club yet to be uncovered—a convivial place for telling stories, killing time, and being one of the boys.

1951 USGA Amateur Championship Poster

The gallery at the 1951 USGA Amateur Championship

Middle left to right: Club founder Eugene Grace, (wearing the hat) and Pat Pazzetti. Front left to right: Cotton Young and Grace's son, Charles Grace of the USGA

Caddie Shack

WHEN APPROACHING SAUCON'S caddie shack, the telltale sign of looper habitation is evident—a trash receptacle filled to overflowing with equal parts stogie stubs and cigarette butts. In some respects, Cotton fits into this setting like a hand in a glove; in other ways, he's miles from the typical caddie stereotype. For instance, he loves taking a crack at Lady Luck on the slots in Atlantic City, and hardly a day goes by without a lottery ticket purchase (his brother once won the $1 million jackpot!), but you'd never find Cotton contributing to the pile-up of stubs and butts. When the Surgeon General released a 1963 report officially linking cigarette smoking to various health ailments, he straightaway kicked his 30-year, pack-a-day habit. In fact, he remembers the exact day, because it happened to fall on his first grandson's birthday, October 27, 1963. This was the best gift Pop-Pop could have given to the newborn—as if Cotton was acknowledging that this new life had given him yet another incentive to stay healthy.

Cotton's first task when entering the caddie shack, his home away from home, is to make a careful inspection, stopping to adjust a picture that is hanging a hairbreadth off center. When finished, he nods with satisfaction, as though he were straightening up his own living room. Since caddying introduced a whole new world to Cotton, he feels an obligation to take care of the place that played a part in enriching his life so profoundly. Having spent an incalculable amount of hours in this humble abode, Cotton says, "I have a lotta memories packed into these four walls."

As you wander around Saucon's caddie shack, you see a wall adorned with a plaque honoring Morry Holland, Saucon's beloved assistant golf professional from 1952-1995. Cotton was obviously quite fond of Holland. Never at a loss for classic golf stories, Cotton picked up where the plaque leaves off. "On the 501-yard, par-5, 4th hole of the Grace course Mr. Holland shot the only double eagle I *ever* witnessed using his trusty 4-iron." A double eagle,

Cotton explains, is rarer than a hole-in-one, because a hole-in-one requires one perfect shot, but a double eagle requires two. "That was the day Mr. Holland set the club record on the Grace Course in the early 1970s with a 64, which is eight strokes under par," says Cotton with admiration. This record-setting round including the endangered golf species— the double eagle—is legendary among the people who witnessed it, for it was unforgettable golf.

"As far as I'm concerned, Mr. Holland was the greatest teacher of golf in the Lehigh Valley," Cotton boasts. In 1986 Holland was named the Philadelphia PGA Section Teacher of the Year. When Cotton is asked about the secret of Holland's success, he says without hesitation, "Mr. Holland just had the knack to figure out a player's strengths and weaknesses and build a golf swing around them. He taught tour pros like Debbie Massey, Holly Vaughn, Jim Booros and plenty of others, and even has a practice range at Saucon named after him," Cotton says, as proud of Holland's accomplishments as if they were his own.

It has been said that golf's perfect round is the impossible dream. Though Cotton agrees, he thinks Holland may have been the closest to achieving this unattainable goal when he shot eight threes and a four, an amazing seven birdies for a 28 on the back nine of the Old Course. "That's the best nine holes I've ever witnessed. You won't find any scorecards proving it though," Cotton laughs, "because Mr. Holland, who was the assistant pro, refused to turn in the scores. He was afraid Ralph Hutchison, the head professional, wouldn't appreciate the numbers. After all, the assistant should never play better golf than his boss." The only remaining evidence of this little known round is Cotton's vivid and detailed recap of Holland's play on the back nine that warm summer day.

History prevails in the caddie clubhouse, and aside from Holland's worthy prominence, commemorative photos of Cotton's induction into the Professional Caddie Association's Hall of Fame and framed newspaper articles featuring Cotton's career accomplishments seem to take center stage on the caddie shack walls.

Just inside the door and to the right in the modest, rectangular room, you'll find tan lockers lining the wall. A locker with Cotton's name on it is filled with memorabilia dating as far back as the 1950s. Under his caddie gear, you'll find a Christmas card featuring a black velvet poodle with a bright, red bow sent from the pet of one-time Bethlehem Steel Vice-President Robert McMath.

Cotton is clearly amused as he recalls this as "the only Christmas card I ever got from a dog." McMath's French standard poodle was named Vicky and was often chauffeur-driven to and from the country club.

Along with the sweet, there are also some bitter memories, like the yellowing newspaper article detailing the death of one of his brothers in an elevator accident and numerous thank-you notes from now-deceased members for whom he will never caddie again.

Another pile includes a newspaper clipping announcing his 50th wedding anniversary, the 80th birthday cards signed by dozens of club members and fading scorecards of particularly memorable rounds like the 1987 PA PGA Michelob Open when his player, Roy Vucinich, shot Cotton's age at the time—71—two days in a row. Cotton boasts, "Mr. Vucinich shot 20 pars and nine birdies." Vucinich's dazzling flurry of birdies won him second place in the tournament, and later he went on to win on the Senior Tour. The lingering presence of these items in Cotton's locker is evidence that he still clings to the golden memories of glories past.

Rummaging through his locker seems to trigger even more nostalgia and Cotton spills over with memories of the men with whom he caddied who eventually went onto to pursue other professions. One such person is Cotton's lawyer, Chester Reybitz, who looped with Cotton over forty years ago. "We played cards together," Cottons says. "He's a great guy who usually hasn't charged me whenever I've needed legal advice."

Toward the back of the caddie shack is a table strewn with playing cards. Rumor has it that this is where caddies play poker on rainy days—a rumor to which Cotton pleads The Fifth. "It's against the rules," he says. Because he's not prone to telling, he doesn't want to say more. Finally, and it isn't easy, he breaks down and concedes to playing two-cent rummy in the early days of his caddie career—hardly a true confession of a high stake poker game.

Built-in seating surrounds the table as well as the perimeter of the caddie shack. Cotton speaks glowingly of these seats as if they were the greatest in creature comforts. He credits Gene Mattare, Saucon's director of golf since 1991, for the upgraded atmosphere. "He's the best thing that ever happened to Saucon caddies—the only pro to ever give us bonuses."

Cotton was the first person Mattare met when he came to Saucon. He describes Cotton as "the dean of caddies with a terrific work ethic, a real gentleman who truly enjoyed his profession. He is regarded with the utmost respect by both caddie and member alike." "Further evidence of his popularity," says Mattare, "is that if Cotton was called ahead of the other caddies, and he usually was, few if any of the others ever said anything about it." This last accolade was no small feat, for though Cotton was the favored choice of many of Saucon's members, most agree that his popularity didn't diminish the camaraderie he enjoyed with his peers. Friend and fellow looper, Larry Taglang, says, "There were only a few disgruntled caddies over the years who were jealous when Cotton was chosen ahead of them for a loop."

When asked about Cotton's most outstanding skill as a veteran caddie, Mattare says, "It is definitely his ability to read the greens—and some of them can be pretty tricky. The 11th hole on the Old Course is like an inverted turtle shell—an optical illusion. Everyone has a hard time with it, including tour players." Once, while Mattare was playing that hole, Cotton said to him, "Everything always breaks toward those trees." Then Cotton, deferring to his player as was his custom, stood on the side of the green and just looked at the putt. Mattare asked, "Cotton, what do you think?" He replied, "Left and center." Mattare wouldn't normally have chosen this strategy, but did so on Cotton's recommendation.

"Boy, he was dead on," recounts Mattare. "He's always on. You expect caddies to give distances and hard facts, but Cotton doesn't even have to get behind the ball to read the greens." Now every time Mattare plays the 11th hole on the Old Course he hears Cotton's voice ringing in his memory, saying, "Everything always breaks towards those trees."

The caddie shack was home to many colorful characters over the years with names like Bubba, Gaylord, Cigar, and Sneezy making up the caddie fraternity. Every Monday for decades, their caddie bond was forged by sharing beers and stories at the Old Colesville Hotel (now The Manor House) after caddying a round or two of golf.

Saucon caddies range in age from college kids to old bones. On a recent visit to the caddie shack, peering from among the shadows in the farthest corner was one young looper lying down on the cushioned bench. An old-timer was using a pocketknife to manicure his fingernails. Both were still hoping to pick up a round for the afternoon. For most caddies, waiting to pick up a loop is a way of life.

Cotton was regarded among his fellow loopers as the gold standard for Saucon caddies. Though a veteran looper at Saucon for 50 years, Cigar recalls

Cotton showing him the ropes as a novice caddie back in the "semi-olden days" of the 1950s. By then, Cotton already had 25 years of caddying under his belt. Cigar (who has likely smoked more stogies than Groucho Marx and first lit up at age 13, thus earning his colorful nickname) says, "Cotton always got the choice of loops." Another caddie, Kevin Nicolas, confirms this claim, saying, "He was among the hottest caddies going. Some days he actually had to hide, he was in such demand." At times, Cotton almost couldn't keep up with member's requests, forcing him to hop from bag to bag—and this was the era when 200 to 300 caddies were tugging for rounds at Saucon.

Until the mid-20th century, club caddies were a part of the landscape of golf courses around the country. This was about to change, however, because of the invention of the motorized golf cart. The carts provided a welcome convenience to golfers lacking the stamina to walk three to four miles of fairways. For some clubs, renting these carts generated new revenue. Quickly, the electric or gas-powered carts changed the livelihoods of club caddies forever—that is, except for Cotton. Maintaining such a large staff of caddies at Saucon was no longer necessary, because some members now opted for a cart rather than a caddie, but Cotton never lacked for a loop.

It should be noted that the number of caddies at Saucon rarely fell under the 75 mark. The club has always been mindful of preserving the time-honored tradition of caddying and even promotes the use of caddies among its members. "In 2004, cart usage was down by 12 percent and caddie usage up by 6 percent," says Mattare who believes caddies are part of the history and tradition of both the game and the club. "Golfers are truly missing out if they don't play with a caddie." Golf without caddies? Perish the thought.

The one and only time that Cotton didn't tote members' clubs was during a caddie strike in the 1930s when loopers refused to work until their wages were increased. They eventually won, and the minimum rate per round went from 55 cents to 90 cents. In 2005, a Saucon "honor" caddie makes $35 a bag, plus tip. A Saucon caddie generally works three loops a week during a 30-week year and makes more in one day than Cotton would have made in a whole year in 1929.

The Great Depression of the 1930s brought with it lean times at Saucon. Still, dedicated club members helped bear the financial burden during a season when many clubs simply shuttered their doors. Taking a creative approach to survival, it wasn't uncommon for management to show movies at night or offer Sunday dinners at the club. These were among the ways Saucon was able to hold onto its membership. "During the hard times, some caddie's shirts were worn out at the shoulder from the friction generated by the bags," Cotton laments. Money was just too scarce for replacements.

In 1937, like most Bethlehemites, Cotton, now 22 years old, started working at Bethlehem Steel full-time as a shipper and saw operator in addition to looping 18 holes five days a week. He tells of a bitter memory, "I loaded up metal destined for Japan, previous to the attack on Pearl Harbor...the very metal they would one day use against us." Bethlehem Steel unwittingly provided raw material for America's future enemy in the Pacific by selling iron and metal to Japan in 1936. It wasn't until 1940 that the United States shut off all exports of war-essential goods to the imperialistic nation. Ironically, company posters referring to Japan and encouraging wartime production efforts later read, "America Needs Ships to Sink the Rising Sun. Let's Go Bethlehem!"

Yet for a day or so in 1938, more Americans were worried about the U.S. being invaded by Martians than they were about the escalating violence in

Europe and Asia, thanks to Orsen Welles' convincing radio broadcast "War of the Worlds."

All Americans of "the greatest generation," a phrase coined by NBC news anchor Tom Brokaw in a book by the same name, remember listening to the radio on December 7, 1941 and hearing: "We interrupt this program to bring you a special news bulletin. The Japanese have just bombed Pearl Harbor." The sudden arrival of war produced acute shortages of manpower affecting all of America, but particularly Bethlehem. There was never a time in American history before or since when so many people were involved in so many ways in a shared cause—in a common effort for the greater good. It was impossible not to be affected in some manner by the war, however far you may have been from the front lines. Though four of Cotton's brothers went to war—two were awarded The Purple Heart—Cotton was given a deferment because of his employment with Bethlehem Steel. With a sense of purpose and patriotism, he proudly and determinedly went to work with the conviction that The Steel's contribution played a critical role in assuring U.S. victory.

During both World Wars, in order to avoid military service, baseball pros flocked to Bethlehem Steel for deferment. When a work-or-fight order was issued by the War Department in WWI, players employed by Bethlehem Steel included "Shoeless" Joe Jackson of the Chicago White Sox and "The Sultan of Swat" Babe Ruth, record-setting *pitcher* for the Boston Red Sox. Of course, Babe was later to become one of the greatest hitters of all time.

As the largest supplier of steel for allied forces during WWII, Bethlehem Steel needed to secure every possible able-bodied worker. When Saucon experienced its own shortage of men due to the war effort, Cotton was "drafted" for a one year "tour" as caddie master all the while maintaining long hours at The Steel. "The closest I ever got to military service," Cotton jokes today, "was marching in 'army golf': LEFT, LEFT, LEFT, RIGHT, LEFT after my players' shank balls."

With all of its loss, WWII did revive prosperity in America and at the Saucon Valley Country Club. Mandatory gas rationing, however, threatened trips to the golf course. The solution? Buses were chartered to transport members to nearby Friedensville. Saucon then hired a horse and wagon to take them the rest of the way. Cotton recalls with cinematic vividness the welcome sound of clattering horses' hooves (*clip-clop, clip clop*) making their way into the club pulling a wagon teeming with members. "We loved to

hear that noise," Cotton beams. "It meant our players
were on their way."

Caddying provided a freedom that Cotton relished.
He blissfully traded the confines of working indoors
for basking on the sunny fairways. Shipping steel
could not compare to the joy of hauling hickories.
Grateful to his profession, Cotton remarks, "I can't
think of many jobs that would have given me the
same chance. After my shift at Bethlehem Steel, I'd
flag a ride [hitchhike] to the club to pick up a loop.
We had badges, so people knew we were caddies and
would feel safe enough to give us a ride. My days
often started before dawn and ended after dark."
Cotton always thought there was something magical
about finishing a golf round as shadows crept across
the 18th fairway at dusk. In 40 years, he missed fewer
days of work at the steel plant than you could count
on one hand, a notable accomplishment considering
the severe snowstorms of yesteryear and the fact that
he didn't own a car until halfway through his career.
He retired in 1977 at the age of 62 and returned to
looping full-time, toting two bags for at least 18
holes.

Some describe caddies as "underpaid and over-
privileged." In years gone by, caddies were generally
too poor to own their own golf equipment, yet willing

Saucon members would often sign off their own clubs from storage for caddies to use. Cotton borrowed the clubs of a prominent and generous member for whom he regularly caddied, Frank Brugler, then vice-president of Bethlehem Steel. He used them for play on Mondays and in tourneys. In fact, it was with Mr. Brugler's lucky clubs that he was match champion in the Fountain Hill Republic Golf Championship in 1964. Later on, Morry Holland gave Cotton the first set of clubs he could call his own.

Every year in July, Saucon hosts a caddie golf tournament. The tourney winner receives not only accolades from his peers but also a coveted trophy at a picnic that follows. Held in the tree-lined caddie yard where loopers can play some hoops or lounge at picnic tables while waiting to pick up a round, the annual event is replete with prizes. These are donated in part by Saucon members to thank caddies and to distinguish exceptional service over the previous year. It was at the first caddie picnic in 1994 that Cotton was awarded a gold watch to honor his many years of dedicated service to the Saucon Valley Country Club. It was at another picnic in 1995 that Cotton received the surprise—and one of the highest honors—of his life. Caddie Master John Suder and Director of Golf Gene Mattare presented him with a plaque inscribed with the words "The Ross 'Cotton' Young Caddie Tournament" immortalizing Cotton's place in Saucon's caddie pantheon forever. Ever since that day, Cotton has proudly participated in presenting the trophy that bears his name to its worthy recipient.

Every time Cotton set out to caddie, he set out in search of untold stories. So on rainy days when the guys take refuge in the caddie shack, Cotton does most of the talking, recounting one great golf yarn after another. Sometimes he'll recall the day he goaded Saucon member and lawyer Tommy Maloney with the challenge: "In 70 years, I've only seen one eagle on the seventh hole on the Old Course." Maloney, taking the bait replied, "I'll do it—*today.*" His eyes lighting up with the memory, Cotton exclaims, still in disbelief, "And he actually did it! That very day he hooked the ball right into the hole for an eagle on No. 7!" Other times Cotton will tell about the 1993 Member-Guest Tournament when Roger White and Ted Taddie shot four birdies on four of the par-4 holes—and pars on all four of the par-3 holes on the Weyhill course, for a total of eight natural threes. Another crowd favorite is the time he looped for a husband and wife foursome and one of the men hit a hole-in-one on the 4th hole. Unbelievably, ten holes later the *other* man of the foursome hit a hole-in-one on No. 14. This amazing round of golf was recorded in *Ripley's Believe It or Not*...and the stories just keep flowing from Cotton like water in a spring-fed reservoir.

So what do caddies talk about in the caddie shack other than golf? Cotton replies in his characteristically raspy voice, "Baseball, of course!" as if the answer should have been self-evident. He has been a loyal Yankees fan for as long as he could pronounce the word and frequented Yankee Stadium several times a year. Cotton has witnessed his share of thrilling baseball moments, like the time Babe Ruth and Lou Gherig *both* hit a home run in the same game. He remembers the remarkable occasion when Yankees' shortstop Tony Lazerri hit a triple with the bases loaded and followed it up with two home runs, also with the bases loaded—that's 11 runs in all! Lazerri led his team to a 25-2 victory over the Philadelphia Athletics, or "A's." In another game of fierce rivalry, James Foxx of the A's hit two home runs off of Yankee pitcher "Lefty" Gomez in the same game. "One to the right field stands, one to the left," Cotton says with a chuckle, "As if Foxx wanted 'to rub it in' to as many Yankee fans as he possibly could."

Cotton's compatriots are fellows whose histories, like his own, are intertwined with the Saucon Valley

Country Club. For 77 years, the caddie shack at Saucon has been much more than just the place where Cotton reported to work or a cavernous clubhouse for overgrown boys, but rather a ripe setting for captivating stories, priceless camaraderie and indelible memories.

Saucon Valley Country Club's caddie shack with its Georgian red brick clubhouse in the background

Fairway Friends

WHEN YOU'VE CADDIED for thousands of players spanning nine decades, answering the question, "Who is your all-time-favorite golfer?" could be a difficult task. Not for Cotton. He answers without the slightest hesitation, "Mr. Killian!" According to this lifelong looper, no celebrity, famous tour pro, politician or industry giant could hold a candle to him. Cotton has been a fairway companion of the Killian family for over five decades and Bill Killian returns Cotton's compliment, referring to the "grand 'ole guy," as "the finest caddie of all time."

Bill Killian is the son of Paul Killian, one-time vice-president of Bethlehem Steel. Paul and Bill were the first members of the Killian family for whom

Cotton started caddying back in 1954.

Golf created friendships for Cotton that would otherwise be unlikely to exist, just as the game brought Cotton and Killian together. Save for their consuming passion for golf, the two had little else in common. The obsessive nature of golf makes it likely for most players' circle of friends to consist exclusively of golfers. (Cotton realized the full extent of Bill Killian's *golf problem*, and was no doubt happy to be an enabler to his player's addiction.) In Cotton's estimation, there is no better game to enhance a friendship than golf, and the friendship between these two men is living proof.

Many of Cotton's current golf relationships are with those who consider him a fatherly or grandfatherly figure; after all, he started caddying at Saucon before most of the current membership were even born. His enduring friendship with Killian, a man closer to his own age, however, is in marked contrast.

Golf, by its very nature, can challenge even the healthiest of self-esteems. Nothing on earth can provoke losing your composure like a round of golf. Every shot brings with it the possibility of glory or the probability of defeat, and even those not accustomed to using foul language find swearing to be like a reflex on the golf course. Usually genteel and well-mannered players, falling under the mysterious spell of this most frustrating of games, have been known to make uncooperative golf clubs an object of attack. The combination of errant balls and battered egos seem to draw out the worst in a person. In a game where disappointments occur far more frequently than strokes of genius, many golfers claim cursing is the only way to get through a round.

While most members tout the merits of Cotton's "no swearing on the greens" reputation, Killian replies mischievously, "Well, no...Cotton isn't much for profanity—that is, unless he's telling a joke or missing a short putt." Cotton possessed a roguish good humor, taking the opportunity to laugh and make others laugh as much as he possibly could. "It's important for players to keep their sense of humor," says Cotton. "Laughing can actually help a golfer's performance." And like most golfers, Killian could use all the help he could get. In fact, Cotton and Killian's shared sense of humor led his caddie to tell his player a few bawdy jokes on the fairways now and then.

Cotton's jokes were like a balm to an anxious golfer's soul and known to put a smile on even the crankiest of duffers' faces. When his players are in need of comic relief (like after they 4-putt, shank, hook or slice the ball), he begins his jokes in a sober tone, attempting to mask his comedic intent, saying:

Did you hear about the guy who was stranded on a deserted island, all alone for ten years?
Then, one day out of the surf comes this gorgeous woman, wearing a wet suit and scuba gear. She comes up to the guy and says, 'How long has it been since you've had a sub sandwich?'
'Ten years!' he says. She reaches over and unzips a waterproof pocket on her suit and pulls out a sub. He takes it, unwraps the packaging, savors every bite, and says, 'Man, that was good!'
Then she asks, 'How long has it been since you've had a drink of whiskey?' He replies, 'Ten years!' She reaches over, unzips another waterproof pocket on her suit, pulls out a flask and gives it to him. He takes a long swig and says, 'Wow, that's fantastic!'
Then she starts unzipping this long zipper that runs down the front of her wet suit and she says to him, 'And how long has it been since you've had some real fun?'
And the man replies, 'My goodness! Don't tell me that you've got a five-iron in there!'

Private clubs have long been known as bastions of discrimination. If discrimination existed at Saucon, you might think a caddie would be a likely victim, but Cotton makes no mention of it and, in fact, tells an opposite tale when it comes to Bill Killian. One of golf's more enjoyable traditions occurs when finishing the round with your playing companions. That's the time when putts have a tendency to get longer over your favorite brew as you relive the highs and lows of the match. If the pastoral beauty of the greens seemed to call a halt to workaday worries, the after-round drinks most certainly completed the surrender. Unlike most, Killian often chose to include his caddie in this ritual.

"Mr. Killian always insisted on bringing me into the 'Members Only' dining area to have a hamburger and beer together," Cotton says. Though the good cheer behind the door of the 19th hole was forbidden territory for caddies, considering Cotton's reputation, members most likely would not have lifted an eyebrow if he accepted the invitation. At first he considered doing so an unthinkable breach of personal protocol so repeatedly, Cotton would graciously decline. He was never one to expect his long tenure at the club to grant him any special privileges. Repeatedly, Killian would respond by sending over a hamburger and beer to the area designated for caddies. His persistent kindness finally prevailed in the late 1950s when Cotton began a decades-long tradition of dining with Killian after a round, a practice that other members winked at. Since Cotton has always said, "Cold beer helps lubricate a golfer's swing," in theory, he was providing yet another service for his player. When asked how Killian got away with breaking the rules among Saucon staff members, Cotton grins and replies, "He always was a big tipper."

Killian was far different from one notorious member who had a bad reputation for stiffing caddies. One old-timer (who shall remain nameless) remembers that it was not uncommon for 50 caddies to line up hoping for a loop. But when the offending member showed up, suddenly there wasn't a caddie to be found. "All were in hiding," laughs the anonymous source. "Most caddies tend to shy away from low tippers and slow players. And heaven forbid if they're both."

Cotton knows from experience what a generous tip can mean to a hard-working, making-ends-meet person. He is known for tipping servers from 30-80 percent of his check total at the Blue Anchor, his favorite restaurant for over 15 years. Waitresses who serve Cotton his bacon and eggs most mornings can bank on a Christmas bonus every year as well. Cotton's family has also been on the receiving end of his generous nature. As a father three times over, a grandfather nine times over, a great-grandfather another ten times over and a great-great-grandfather once, he has a perfect track record for never forgetting to send a money-filled birthday and Christmas card for all of his progeny.

Bill Killian, known for hosting foursomes, was a successful and influential man with many high-profile friends and associates. Several times a year, Cotton looked forward to the rough-and-tumble foursome competition between Killian and three fellow alumni from Bucknell University. Killian would compensate his caddie handsomely, and despite Cotton's protests, the old college buddies insisted on liberally adding to the kitty. Hands down, caddying for the "Bucknellians" was the highlight of the golf season for Cotton. No matter who had previously requested him to loop on the days Killian came into town, it was understood by all whose bag Cotton would carry.

Along with thoroughly enjoying caddying for these men, Cotton has a theory on the popularity of foursomes. In his opinion, golfers play better as a team than as individuals or coupled in a twosome. "As a player in a foursome, your mind is tricked into playing the same way pros do," claims Cotton. "You stay in the shot—in the present. When standing over a bunker, you don't tense-up because it wasn't your drive that landed the shot in the sand. If you hit a shot that lands in the rough, someone else will have to play the ball from the bad lie. When lining up a putt, there's no reason to worry because the comeback won't be up to you. Wanting to make a shot too much only makes it worse." Playing with the mindset that the outcome doesn't matter is almost preferable to playing with too much concern. Cotton maintains that players do better when they focus on each individual shot as though it's the only one they'll ever have to make.

Unfortunately, there is a disclaimer to this premise. Cotton says none of this applies to foursomes that include married couples, because their tendency to squabble nullifies their ability to take advantage of this winning sports psychology. Occasionally golfers can create this "higher consciousness" while playing solo, because without an audience they are freed from their egos, enabling them to invest their energy entirely in the stroke. "The only trouble with that," Cotton says, "is then you have no witnesses to confirm your claims."

Though Killian lived in the suburbs of Pittsburgh, it wasn't uncommon for him to come into town to play a round of golf and invite Cotton out to the Manor House, a popular, upscale restaurant in Bethlehem. (Ironically, before its renovation, it was the same restaurant that caddies used to frequent in the early days of Cotton's career when it was called the Colesville Hotel.)

One day Cotton caddied for a Killian foursome that included Harlan Hinkle, who was a shipmate of the decorated naval aviator, George Herbert Bush in WWII. Hinkle gave his caddie a photograph of the 41st president standing in front of the presidential seal, signed: "To Ross 'Cotton' Young with best wishes, George Bush." (The former president's affinity for golf inspired a 1,500 square foot addition to the White House by way of a nine-hole practice green. No doubt the 41st president was influenced by his father Prescott Bush, who was elected president of the USGA in 1934, and his maternal grandfather, George Herbert Walker, who was president of the USGA in 1920 and founder of the Walker Cup.)

Rounding out the foursome was Army Football's legendary Heisman Trophy winner and NCAA Hall of Fame player Glen Davis, plus Chuck Bednarik, who played for the Philadelphia Eagles from 1948 to 1962. The term "hero" was appropriate to use when describing Davis and Bednarik, who not only gave their all on the gridiron but also while serving their country in the military. Before the age of specialization in football, "Concrete Charlie," as Bednarik was known, was the last of the "Sixty Minute Men" and "two-way players" who played both offense and defense on game day. What most know about Bednarik is that he was an NFL All-Pro in 1949, 1956 and 1960 and an inductee into the Pro Football Hall of Fame in 1967. A little known fact, however, is that Chuck was a former caddie. Cotton not only caddied for Bednarik but also with him many years earlier. Cotton says, "Chuck Bednarik's hands are so huge they just make the grip of the club disappear."

While it wasn't unusual for Cotton to be in such distinguished company on the greens, it was unusual for him to socialize around a table laden with fine china, sparkling crystal and crisp, white linens. Still, after their match, Cotton was asked to accompany them and their wives at The Manor House for dinner.

Everyone in the group had mixed drinks except for Cotton, who ordered a beer. Finding the menu somewhat daunting, Cotton, who embodies simplicity, made no attempt to bluff or pretend knowledge of cuisine he did not possess. It didn't occur to him to be intimidated. He requested Salisbury steak, a familiar comfort food that happened to be his favorite. This fine dining establishment had every cut of prime meat imaginable on the menu, but Salisbury steak was not one of them. Killian intervened and made sure

Cotton got just what he wanted.

In the years that followed, Cotton made repeated visits to the restaurant and requests for Salisbury steak. Eventually, Jim Duke, owner of The Manor House and Saucon member finally said, "Cotton, you are really going to have to expand your palate." A man without disguises and unapologetic for who he is, Salisbury steak still remains the clear front-runner of Cotton's culinary picks today.

When Killian was "roasted" on special occasions marking milestones in his life, friends and colleagues never failed to mention stories of the honoree and his faithful caddie. The teasing testimonials often went like this: "Cotton would give us a warm and respectful greeting—and then we never saw him again until the 18th hole! Why, you might ask? Because he was busy running all over the course searching for Killian's errant balls." Though the crowd would laugh heartily, Cotton was quick to defend Killian's golfing reputation when he would hear of the jokes.

One of the most addicting athletic experiences known to man is the simple act of blasting the ball off the tee and having it land anywhere near its intended target. Satisfaction isn't guaranteed—it's fleeting at best—but it's enough to make a visceral impression. The next pure shot becomes something to seek, seemingly at any cost. On the rare occasion, even an ordinary golfer can pull off a stroke of cerebral, muscular and anatomical harmony that would make a tour pro proud—yes, even if your given name happens to be Eldrick.* The disparity between the ordinary golfer and the pro is that ordinary golfers' good shots, not their bad, are the ones viewed as inexplicable.

All the conditions for the happy union of ball and sweet spot seemed optimal one fine day as caddie and player approached the par-4, dogleg-right, 3rd hole (now No. 13) on the Weyhill Course. Cotton was looping for Killian's grandson, Ryan. Throughout the successive generations that he has caddied for the family, Ryan became one of Cotton's favorites. Amid congenial company, blue skies and no wind, Cotton recommended Ryan go for the green—an invisible target hidden behind a tall stand of pines—with a driver instead of the safer 5-iron to the middle of the fairway. Emboldened by his caddie's urgings, Ryan stepped up to the tee, stared down the fairway, fixed his gaze beyond the trees and took a mighty cut, swinging through with power and confidence. The swish of his club had a different sound, a higher pitch than you hear in a standard swing, and at the moment of impact the ball seemed already half way to its target—leaving a hiss in its slipstream. Cotton

* Eldrick "Tiger" Woods

coaxed a shot out of Ryan that he didn't even know he was capable of hitting.

"He aimed for the trees and cleared them," says Cotton. "Ryan nailed the ball with one of the sweetest and most compact swings I'd ever seen. It was a beauty!" The little white sphere seemed possessed of a soul. To those watching, it appeared like the ball flew free from the weight of gravity, dropping in the far green distance. When Cotton reached the probable landing area, Ryan's ball was nowhere to be found, so he questioned a nearby greenskeeper. Remarkably, his ball landed at least five yards beyond the green—and on this par-4 hole, that was an incredible 320 yards.

Inside the psyche of every golfer is a persistent desire to improve, to innovate and to overcome. Most golfers cling to the belief that the perfect swing is only another day or an expensive piece of equipment away. (Mathematically speaking, if all the strokes advertisers told golfers they could save by using their products worked, wouldn't they all be shooting in the negative numbers by now?) But Ryan, for one day on the 3rd hole, found his illustrious, elusive, and mysterious swing. In all of his years of caddying, Cotton had never seen a shot sail so far—and there has never been a caddie more proud.

Cotton claims, "If you really want to know a person, get out on the course with them a few times." This speaks volumes about the familiarity between Cotton and Killian, who have walked the course together since the year Boeing unveiled the 707, the first kidney was transplanted, McCarthyism ran rampant and the Supreme Court ruled that racial segregation in public schools was unconstitutional. Theirs was a friendship that spanned summers, decades, even a lifetime, enduring through the best and worst of times. For more than half a century, Cotton and Killian have tightly held onto a simple love of the game that has sealed their fairway friendship.

One day Cotton observed an elderly but determined man practicing his drive. His short, turn-less swing was the product of compromise between desire, old bones and stiff muscles. Someone made the comment, "He's hitting them pretty good." Cotton smiled and murmured with his special brand of humor, "Good, because he's running out of time!" Only a golfer of a certain vintage could get away with a joke like this.

Outside of the world of golf, Killian and Cotton have another common bond; they share the challenges of growing old together, willing allies in their battle against the calendar. Killian does not make it to Saucon as often these days, but when he does, Cotton still mans the cart. Though the yips may affect their putting strokes and on some days even a golf cart seems like too much effort, Cotton and Killian's enduring friendship helps ease their face-off with Father Time. Perhaps there is an up side to the older guy's game. Their shots may not go very far, but then again, the caddie never has to search for the ball.

Cotton with his fairway friend
of 51 years, Bill Killian

The Looper and His Ladies

THOUGH WOMEN HAVE PLAYED a large part in the history of golf, their first few hundred years are mostly clouded in anonymity. Women certainly played the sport, but because of a strong bias toward male players, woman golfers are not mentioned in many early writings.

One of the first known golfers of either sex back in the mid-1500s was Mary, Queen of Scots. In France, where Mary grew up, military cadets not only provided security but also carried golf clubs for royalty, and it is likely that Mary first introduced the custom of caddying.

Mary, an avid player, was not only the first noted, but also the most notorious of female golfers. She caused a scandal when seen playing the game at St. Andrews within days of her husband's mysterious murder. There was rather strong suspicion that Mary was a conspirator to the murder though it was never quite proven. Mary herself was ultimately beheaded at age 44 after being accused of plotting against the life of Queen Elizabeth I of England.

In years past a female's path to the golf course was paved with male resistance. In the 19th century, golf was mostly a gentleman's game although a few ladies were grudgingly allowed to participate. During the era when women wore confining combinations of corsets, high collars, and petticoats, golf was actually seen as a way for the "weaker sex" to get exercise without over-exertion. The strength of mind the game demanded was perceived to be a helpful way to bolster "unsteady female emotions."

Some purported that GOLF was actually an acronym for Gentlemen Only Ladies Forbidden—an idea discounted by historical record. Initially, however, many country clubs were dubbed "Eveless Edens" and were exclusively the domain of men. Women were refused admittance into the clubhouses and were forced to submit to restricted tee times. The prevailing attitude was one of condescension. An observer by the name of Lord Wellwood, near the close of the

19th century noted, "If women choose to play when the male golfers are feeding or resting, no one can object; at other times, they are in the way."

During this era, women were expected *not* to take a full swing and stick only to "lady-like" strokes such as chipping and putting. When the Ladies Golf Union held their first championship at Royal Lytham and St. Annes Golf Club in 1893, a British official objected that "constitutionally and physically, women are unfit for golf." He then forecasted "that the first ladies championship would be their last." He was wrong, of course. In 2000, the Ladies Professional Golf Association (LPGA) celebrated their 50th anniversary. The LPGA today is a prosperous organization of 34 tournaments with approximately $40 million in purses per year.

The women's next obstacle to a full golf swing was the corset, a device designed to narrow a women's waist to 13, 12, 11, and even ten or less inches. Fashionable ladies deemed it as a necessary undergarment from the 1550s to the early 20th century, starting when Catherine de Medici, wife of King Henry II of France, enforced a ban on thick waists at court. Millions of women breathed a collective (and literal) sigh of relief when the U.S. Industries Board called on women to stop buying corsets in 1917. The years of whalebones, steel rods and midriff torture came to an end for the purpose of freeing up 28,000 tons of metal for the war effort. In so doing, women's golf swings were freed up as well.

Mildred "Babe" Didrikson Zacharias is credited with putting the LPGA on the map by winning 31 tournaments including three U.S. Opens. Babe is said to be the first woman to hit the ball "like a man." When asked how she accomplished such a feat, she boldly quipped, "By taking off my girdle and beating the ball."

According to the Guinness Book of World Records, Kelly Robbins struck the longest recorded drive by a woman, 429.7 yards at the Elmira Corning Regional Airport in Corning, New York, on May 22, 1995. (The longest recorded drive by a man is 458 yards by Jack Hamm, at Highland Ranch, Colorado on July 20, 1993.)

The first American to win an Olympic gold medal [in golf] was Margaret Abbott, who shot a 47 in the nine-hole final at the 1900 Games in Paris. Abbott told her relatives back in Chicago that she won the tournament, "because the French girls apparently misunderstood the nature of the game and turned up to play in high heels and tight skirts."*

Here's a gender-specific golf mishap for the

record books. In 1983, a Canadian amateur golfer, Elaine Johnson, miss-hit a ball that landed in her own bra. "I'll take a two-stroke penalty," she said. "But I'll be damned if I'll play it where it lies."*

Word has it that the ancient male-only society is collapsing as the wall between men and women golfers crumbles. The British Open, said to be the most sexist championship in the sport, has opened its field to women *if* they qualify. In addition, the British PGA has appointed a woman as its new captain—the very first in its 104-year history!

Woman players have come a long way, baby. Today, according to the National Golf Foundation, they are the sport's fastest growing demographic worldwide. Twenty-five percent of Saucon members are women. When asked who he would rather caddie for—men or women—Cotton answers, "Generally speaking, women." Cotton, always the dapper caddie, is known to be a favorite among the ladies. Part of his appeal as a charismatic fairway figure is undoubtedly his winsome persona and good looks. As noted previously, in his younger years Cotton resembled Robert Redford with his piercing blue eyes and coif of blonde hair. Later on, many thought his greased pompadour and twinkling eyes reminded them of former President Ronald Reagan.

And what is the secret to Cotton's "every hair in place" pompadour? Vaseline Petroleum Jelly is the wonder product that has served to tame his luxuriant mane of white hair since the early 1950s. When one suggests he switch to a modern day hair product like mousse or gel, Cotton maintains, "Vaseline has done just fine for 50 years. No reason to change now." With Cotton's white hair still lush at 89, perhaps Vaseline should be marketed as an elixir to prevent premature hair loss.

Cotton looped for quite a few women pros over the years including long-hitter Holly Vaughn, Debbie Massey (who Cotton witnessed birdie three holes in a row on the Grace Course), Joan Washam (who Cotton says, "couldn't have been more than 110 pounds, but hit the ball 250 yards"), Marilyn Smith, who had numerous career victories on the LPGA circuit and Jerilyn Britz, winner of the LPGA championship and U.S. Women's Open.

None of these women pros, however, could compare to the revolving foursome of ladies Cotton has looped for every Friday for the last ten years. The group includes Myra St. John, Joan McKeon, Mary Brendel, Nancy Norris, Eleanor Workman, Nalda Stevens and Tiki Mershon. This colorful bunch of women is as varied in their personalities and interests as they are in their golf scores. For instance, Mrs. St. John and her husband traveled to Europe in 2004 and sent Cotton a Christmas card with a photo of them wearing fur-lined parkas while visiting an ice bar in Stockholm. Cotton was amused by the card, saying, "It's not every day you know someone who sipped vodka out of glasses made with ice." When St. John isn't traveling, she's learning Spanish, writing her memoirs, rollerblading and of course, golfing.

The camaraderie among the players and their caddie shapes these golf outings. From the first tee off with Cotton on their bags, the Saucon ladies recognized their looper's talent for making a difference in their golf games. Later they realized what a difference he made in their lives.

Myra St. John hosts a birthday party in Cotton's honor every October—a tradition that started nine years ago. At first, embarrassed by the attention, Cotton ducked the ladies' invitations to celebrate his birthday. Just because Cotton was comfortable with them on the greens didn't mean he would be at ease in a round-table social setting. When confronted, he told Mrs. St. John, "I don't want to have a party." Cotton repeats her reply with a laugh. "I don't care what you want," she said. "We're throwing you a party!" And that's just what they did.

Now Cotton looks forward to the big event every year. At the most recent birthday gathering, the women bragged that even at 80 years old, Cotton could still carry two bags at a time, though his pace slowed from a jog to an amble. One day, when Cotton was 81 and no carts were available, he strapped on two bags each stuffed with 25 some odd pounds of golfing equipment and said, "Let's go!" The ladies refused to let him. "We've grown older together along with Cotton. Right about the time that he started using a cart, we started using one, too," said one of the partygoers with obvious affection.

The St. John's lovely home, located in close proximity to Saucon's courses, was the backdrop for Cotton's 89th birthday party. Cotton showed up early wearing his favorite cardigan sweater—the same color of his robin's egg blue eyes—monogrammed with Saucon Valley Country Club's insignia. He sat at the head of the table adorned with his yellow rose boutonniere, enjoying every moment of Myra's gourmet luncheon (though if asked, he likely could not tell you what was on his plate). Cotton was presented a birthday card simply signed, "Fondly, some Saucon Ladies." The homemade card features headlines cut from magazines and newspapers with handwritten addendums such as:

Golf Is A Game For Life *"...and you proved it."*

Quick Cures *"...and you've plenty of them."*

Bonus *"...you've always been one."*

Play On Cloud Nine *"...when you're our man."*

It's Not About Gender. It's About Putting A Little Ball In A Little Hole *"...you've always known it."*

Demand A Superior Product *"...that's what you've always given us."*

Cotton has a love-hate relationship with this kind of attention.

Golf is a gentleman's game, and Cotton is a gentleman caddie. In a world where traditions are becoming dispensable and standards are ceasing to exist, Cotton remains the same, holding the core values of golf and his respect for people intact. His manners and grasp of protocol are from another era. He has both a warmth and a reserve that complement each other. While some of the newer caddies desire to call members by their first names, Cotton was old-world schooled and refuses such familiarity. Even after repeated efforts by some to have him address them by their first names, Cotton would smile and go right back to addressing them as Mister or Missis. At some point during the photo-taking session of the birthday festivities, Mrs. St. John tried once again to encourage Cotton to call her Myra—to no avail. In many ways they had become dear friends, and yet there would always be a measure of decorum between them.

Accolades showered on Cotton at his 89th birthday celebration included his reputation as "the great fisherman." One of the ladies noted, "Cotton would fish as many balls from the creek as he could find, then pass them along to us." In actuality, Cotton has retrieved golf balls out of just about every conceivable place in service to the Saucon ladies over the years. He has chivalrously dredged them out of the creek, pried them out of the ground and searched for them in the rough.

His expertise stems back to his early days of looping, before the era of the 12-foot long ball retriever, when the "creek boy" (pronounced *crick* boy) would earn ten cents for every ball he recovered. "Everyone wanted to be the creek boy," Cotton says with a mischievous look in his eyes, "because you could earn *far* more than a caddie." The reason? When Cotton's turn to be creek boy came up, the first thing he did was move the markers to the rear of the tee to make sure that more balls than usual would go into the water. He did this with the exception of one member, who always paid extra to the creek boy if he hit the ball *over* the creek. When Cotton saw him coming, he would quickly move the markers forward to make sure his man got over the water in the first shot.

The ladies claim Cotton's acumen wasn't limited to the greens. In addition to having an eagle eye and being the best reader of greens in the world, he could read women equally well. A great caddie is both knowledgeable and sensitive—and never offers input when it is not welcome. Once Cotton sensed that his input was appreciated, he would diplomatically help players correct or improve their swings. He was known, however, to be most audacious with Myra St. John, who heartily welcomed his constructive criticism. After a particularly bad shot, he'd shake his head in a teasing, good-natured way and say, "That was no good, Mrs. St. John." As for her response to Cotton's assessment, she says, "Cotton is very special to me, and when he corrects my game, I have a very daughterly feeling toward him."

Ever protective of the fragile golf psyche, Cotton kept score but often held the numbers back until the very end so that the ladies' nerves wouldn't affect their games. He was known to "tally scores quicker than a calculator" and today suggests with a hint of pride that his "great-grandson, David, gets his smarts from me." (David is currently studying microbiology specializing in immunology and virology for his Ph.D. at the Penn Sate College of Medicine.)

The wonder of golf is its self-imposed agony, especially when it comes to the super self-imposed misery of putting. Every ball either stops short or rolls long with the cup looking barely large enough to hold the flagstick. You imagine a perfectly executed putt, one that you've made a dozen times without a miss when no one's watching. The one time you want to make it—the one time it really matters—it comes up short. The sound of the ball rattling in the cup is only a vague and distant memory. You want to plead with the others in your foursome, "I made that putt! It just didn't go in! I've made it from that distance a dozen times running without a miss!" But, alas, there is no escaping the immediate and clearly evident results, nor the blame that falls squarely and solely on the golfer's shoulders. The walk to the next tee offers ample opportunity for reflection, dejection, recrimination—the perfect sunny day turns to storm clouds in the golfer's soul. This, too, is the domain of the faithful caddie. Cotton, gentle in nature, managed to put it all into perspective for his ladies by saying, "Take your swing seriously, but best not take *yourself* too seriously." His homespun philosophy combined with his wise, blue eyes somehow brought comfort when golfers felt cheated by old man par.

Many players believe that having an experienced, supportive caddie on your side makes a difference, not only helping to lower your score but also making the game more enjoyable. "We played as much for Cotton as we played for ourselves," the ladies unanimously agree. "We always did better when Cotton was on our bags." "My husband was my first love, but Cotton is my second," adds Tiki Mershon.

When asked what his favorite era for caddying was, would Cotton's answer be the prime of his life during the 1951 Amateurs? Or perhaps it was his week in the spotlight at the 1992 U.S. Senior Open? Cotton, without hesitation, replies, "The last 10 years when I caddied regularly for the ladies." If, as some say, golf's main attractions are the company you keep and the memories you make, this revolving foursome of ladies and their caddie embody the best of both.

The gentleman caddie and some of his lady players, From left: Mary Brendel, Nancy Norris, Cotton, Myra St. John and Nalda Stevens

The looper and his ladies at one of his annual birthday celebrations

Men of Steel

INTEGRAL TO THE STORY surrounding Cotton's life is the Bethlehem Steel Corporation. Known locally as "The Steel," the mills produced essential materials that forged victories against tyranny for America and our allies in two global wars. Eugene Grace was the man at the helm during this golden era industrial age. Starting as a crane operator, he rose through the ranks to run the massive company. The Bethlehem Steel Corporation was founded in 1904 by Charles M. Schwab and descended from a 19th century iron company. While Schwab, the former president of Carnegie Steel Company, created The Steel, it was Grace's skill and drive that formed it into both the nation's second largest steelmaker and its number one shipping company. Together their combined leadership created one of the greatest companies to ever stamp its mark on world history—all this, despite its humble inception in an obscure and tiny Moravian village.

Over the course of Eugene Grace's four-decade tenure as president of The Steel, one of his greatest exploits was the company's contribution to U.S. military strength during World War I as the largest supplier of arms for Allied forces. Dedicated steel workers labored day and night building ships and munitions, stepping up their efforts significantly after the United States joined the fight in April 1917.

The Steel was not limited to fabricating the guns and ships of war. Its workers also produced the innovative "H" beams that revolutionized building construction and made skyscrapers possible. From sea to shining sea, The Steel permanently transformed America's landscape with buildings and bridges, the likes of which had never been seen before. New York City's skyline was framed by Bethlehem steel in structures such as the Chrysler and Woolworth buildings, the Waldorf-Astoria Hotel and the George Washington Bridge. The Steel was also responsible for building the skeletons of the Benjamin Franklin Bridge in Philadelphia and San Francisco's famed Golden Gate Bridge.

Still, there was nothing sports enthusiast Eugene Grace enjoyed more than to leave the executive boardroom for the fairways of the Saucon Valley Country Club. Steel production and golf were Grace's two passions, and he was said to have been as intense about the one as he was the other. Ironically, when Grace was first captivated by the game of golf in 1909, steel shafts had not yet made their debut on the fairways. First introduced in the U.S. in 1925, the earliest steel shafts were coated to resemble hickory to help ease consumer transition. By the mid-1930s, they were standard everywhere. For Grace, it likely came as no surprise that steel shafts were superior to hickory. The innovative steel clubs were produced with greater uniformity and had a diminished tendency to break, but perhaps best of all, players could hit the ball farther. The 1920s also marked a shift to less nostalgic names assigned to golf clubs. Only an old-timer would remember terms like cleek, spoon, mashie, jigger and niblick—a far cry from today's familiar numbering system.

No one enjoys waiting for a tee time and Grace, who was not accustomed to waiting for anything, was no exception. In 1920, Grace's abhorrence for time wasting inspired his next great accomplishment. He set his sights on a 208-acre farm, and then set about to establish the Saucon Valley Country Club. Eugene Grace and his associates could think of no better way to help promote The Steel's corporate identity. As with most of Grace's dreams, this too became a reality. Rallying around the vision, those first members recruited their wives and even their children to clear stones, dismantle pigsties and tear down chicken coops. One of the greatest challenges was to convert the 200-year-old farmhouse into a clubhouse.

In 1938, the same year the USGA decided to limit to 14 the number of clubs players carried on the course (much to every caddie's delight), war broke out in Europe, resulting in orders for steel pouring in to Bethlehem from Britain. On September 3, 1939, two days after Adolf Hitler's invasion of Poland, Britain and France declared war on Germany. A Saucon caddie conveyed the news to Grace and his golf partners (who happened to be Steel executives) during tee off, and as the story goes, Grace said, "Gentlemen, we are going to make some money."

And make money they did. The nation rapidly geared itself for mobilization of its people and its entire industrial capacity. Exceeding the already notable steel production of WWI by far, The Steel produced 73 million tons of steel for WWII. Company yards built 380 ships in one year, surpassing Grace's enormously aggressive goal of one ship a day. Bethlehem Steel alone built one-fifth of the U.S. Navy's two-ocean fleet. America was united and actively supported the war, and The Steel workers' fervor was fueled by an unwavering conviction that their contribution played a critical role in assuring victory. Completely absorbed in their monumental challenge, there seemed to be no stopping this steel plant as its workers, numbering into the hundreds of thousands, sealed America's role as the great arsenal of democracy. At one point, Bethlehem Steel recorded 283,765 workers on the payroll during WWII. The Steel extended its reach across the country and beyond to include other plants as well as railroads, mines and shipyards. A 1941 *Fortune* magazine article stated that Bethlehem "has geared every unit of its empire to a functional efficiency that Adolf Hitler would envy."

Grace became the highest-paid corporate executive in America, with average annual earnings of $600,000 over 20 years beginning in 1918. (Even Elbert Gary, chairman of mammoth U.S. Steel, never made more than $500,000 a year.) In 1929, the year the stock market on Wall Street crashed, Grace's combined salary and bonuses equaled over $1.6 million. In 1945, during Grace's chairmanship, the assets of The Steel were $881 million; revenue was $1.3 billion, and net income was $34.9 million.

Though described as pleasant, charming and courteous, Grace's imperious nature also made him someone you dare not cross. Legend has it that The Steel, which maintained its own police force and fire department, used to take responsibility for plowing the snow on Bethlehem streets in winter. This generous pursuit continued until a rift occurred between Grace and the mayor. Following that altercation, Grace told the city (which had little or no snow removal equipment) that from then on, Bethlehem would have to take care of snow removal on its own.

Because Bethlehem was at the center of the industrial universe, there were few limits to the power and influence of this steel tycoon. Eugene Grace, at the zenith of his Steel power, refused to travel to Washington for a meeting with the President but insisted instead that Franklin D. Roosevelt come to him. In sharp contrast, this same man *personally* drove his caddie home from the Saucon course after a round of golf.

Cotton says, "Before Mr. Grace started using a chauffeur, he would drive me home in his 12-cylinder black Packard. In the 1930s, there were very few cars and only two traffic lights in Bethlehem." Cotton chuckles as he recalls, "Mr. Grace never bothered to stop at or even slow down for the lights. The first time it happened, I said to him, 'Mr. Grace, you went through a red light!' He replied, 'What red light?'" Eugene Grace became the star of dozens of Cotton's anecdotes.

In the book authored by Grace's granddaughter, Penny Porter, *Eugene Gifford Grace—1876-1960: As We Remember Him*, Porter describes a similar scenario:

> At 3 p.m. every day, the horn blasted at the steel mill announcing it was time to go home...Outside the office building, his brown Cadillac waited. And the moment he was seated behind the wheel, the Bethlehem Police Department was alerted to watch for the safety of motorists and pedestrians who might make the mistake of crossing his path. Officers were dispatched to every traffic light between the plant, Five Points (in south Bethlehem, where Wyandotte, Broadway and Dakotah streets meet), and the highway leading to the golf course. No red light was permitted to slow Mr. Grace's progress to his beloved golf game at Saucon...Legend assures us he drove 50 mph through every intersection.

Another story that still circulates among Saucon old-timers is when Grace, after finishing his round, got in his car to go home. Golf Pro Ralph Hutchison hurried to the caddie shack and alerted the police, then officers strategically rushed to Five Points, the Hill-to-Hill Bridge and Prospect Avenue to keep Grace's route clear. Everywhere Grace went took on the look of a command center anticipating the arrival of the President.

Cotton reminisces about the times that Grace, as if on auto-pilot, would drive right by Cotton's street directly to his own home—forgetting his caddie was in the car. There could be no confusing the two radically different residences. Grace's mansion contained 23 bedrooms, 15 bathrooms, three greenhouses, a bomb shelter, and of course, a driving range and a putting green with a fleet of servants who kept it running. Cotton's humble abode provided a stark contrast to such luxury, though it was only four blocks away from Grace's Prospect Avenue mansion. (This mansion has long since been converted into the Holy Family Manor Assisted Living Facility.) Cotton, not wishing to disturb Grace, who was obviously immersed in his thoughts, would quietly slip out of the car and walk home.

According to Cotton, Grace was a pretty accomplished golfer, "playing off a three or four handicap." To this day he carries with him the memory of his swing, its fluid power and the stretch into the arc at the finish. He was not, however, the easiest man for whom to caddie. "Mr. Grace wouldn't know if he came up short a case of expensive champagne, but if he was missing even *one* golf ball—look out," exclaims Cotton. The Steel president owned one of the only three battery-operated golf carts that existed in the country, labeled with his initials: EGG. A common complication with the new-fangled contraption was that by the time Grace would get to the 18th hole, there wasn't enough charge left to make it up the hill. Cotton would recruit muscular Saucon members who could be easily found displaying their physiques at the club's swimming pool. Some reluctant "volunteers" would attempt to hide, knowing that they would not only be required to push the cart up the hill, but also push the cart up the hill *with* Grace sitting behind the wheel. When Grace traveled to other courses in other states, so did his golf cart, which was taken there in tow by Steel employees.

This industry leader had been the captain of his college baseball team at Lehigh University. An avid baseball fan, he could rattle off professional players' names and batting averages with the glibness of an expert. He regularly required Cotton to run to the caddie master after nine holes to check on baseball scores.

During a round in the 1960s pitting Grace against

Leroy Lincoln, then chairman of Metropolitan Life, Lincoln boasted that Metropolitan Life was three times larger than Bethlehem Steel. After the last shot on the 18th, Grace told Cotton, "I'll never play with Lincoln again; he talks too much." Grace kept his vow, but that didn't mean he was free from Lincoln's nattering. Leroy enjoyed exploiting Eugene's eccentric wardrobe habits. Cotton says, "Regardless of the temperature or time of year, Mr. Grace always put on his camel-hair topcoat when he left the course." The favorite fairway pants of one of the world's wealthiest men were a bluish-gray color with two big 3x5-inch patches on each "cheek." On one occasion Lincoln was playing in a foursome behind Grace and noticed that his friend wasn't wearing his signature pants. He yelled out, "Hey E.G., I miss the patches on your britches!" Cotton says that, "Mr. Grace was not the least bit impressed."

Adjustments were made to the course at Saucon over the years to make play more challenging—and on occasion, less difficult. According to Cotton, "After the 1951 Amateurs, when Ken Venturi double-eagled for two under par on the first hole, Grace demanded the yardage be increased from 512 to 558 yards." When Grace habitually drove his ball into a tree on the 16th hole, he protested the very existence of the tree and requested that it be cut down...and so it was. On the Old Course's 10th hole, Grace's ball always managed to find the trap on the right hand side. Another "suggestion" from Grace led to the filling in of that vexing trap and the sudden emergence of a new trap on the opposite side—all completed before Grace returned for his next round of golf.

In a sport that esteems honor and honesty and where character is said to be fully revealed, improving a lie is considered the unpardonable sin. It must be noted that rumors of improprieties swirl around Grace's golf game, but when Cotton is confronted with these stories, no answer is forthcoming. While Cotton maintains, "Golf is a contest of honor," he provides no comment to the tale that Grace blasted an unrecoverable shot into a cornfield and the ball "suddenly" appeared out of nowhere with a clear shot to the green. Only his caddie knows...and he's not talking. By Cotton's facial expression, you know that probing further would be futile. One comes away with the feeling that this is just one of many course secrets Cotton will take to the grave.

In 1959, *Business Week* magazine listed six members of Bethlehem Steel's senior management on their list of highest-paid executives in America. The number one spot was held by Steel's CEO, Arthur B. Homer, known for the gas turbines he designed and for leading The Steel's ship construction effort in WWII. Not surprisingly, Cotton caddied for Homer and, in fact, carried the bags of every Bethlehem Steel board chairman and president with the exception of one lone executive who did not golf. After all, it makes sense that men at the top of their industry desired a caddie at the top of his.

By day Cotton worked at The Steel, and whenever possible he was on the greens at Saucon. This was true for The Steel's executives, too. This elite group was expected to live in certain neighborhoods located within minutes of both the company headquarters and the club. The road leading to Saucon was dubbed "Vice-President's Row." Golf on the weekend combined with clubhouse poker afterwards was an obligatory part of the typical executive schedule.

On occasion, Robert McMath, who was vice-president, chairman of the finance committee and "number three man" at The Steel would pull Cotton out of work in the middle of a shift to accompany him on Saucon's greens. For 17 years, Cotton served McMath with his specialized knowledge of the Old Course.

Gambling is a part of the fabric of even recreational golf where a small wager is considered a way to keep things interesting. Exceptional players sometimes prey on the self-delusion of average golfers.

One day on the sprawling Saucon greens, Robert McMath challenged Leroy Lincoln to a $100 wager. With more than money at stake ($100 was a mere token of the fierce competition that existed between two of the great leaders of American business in the 20th century), Lincoln took up the gauntlet. There was no throttling back when he attacked the green with his 5-iron, scarring the earth and lobbing a divot the size of a toupee. While the ball was still in the air, Cotton forecasted—*out loud*—that the wildly off-target shot would hit a specific tree and land in the creek. Lincoln called out to the ball commanding it to avoid the tree, which it completely ignored, unwilling to be talked into submission. The little white orb didn't recognize Lincoln as an authority figure. He tried again with urgings, warnings, and pleas. Nothin'. The ball offered no preferential treatment for the chairman of Metropolitan Life. Lincoln watched in horror as his caddie's prediction came true, and the slow-moving creek swallowed up his ball. Sadly, men of all professions and socioeconomic levels are held hostage to the whims of the tiny white ball. Cotton says, still amused, "Mr. Lincoln was so mad, he refused to talk to me for the rest of the round."

But not to worry, he was back to his old jovial self by the next time he played at Saucon.

Lincoln wasn't known for being a good putter, but his ball fell prisoner to the metal cup once when he sunk a forty-foot putt on the 18th hole. All who witnessed the unlikely event were certain it was accomplished by a fortuitous accident. Continuing the amiable teasing that defined their relationship, Cotton sent Lincoln a huge, 12x12-inch Christmas card that year. At the bottom of the card, Cotton taunted, "You must have had your eyes closed when you made that putt," and simply signed it: "Whitey." To portray the closeness of their relationship, Lincoln was one of two golfers through the years that had his own personal moniker for Cotton, thus the origin of "Whitey"—another reference to the caddie's trademark blonde hair.

Robert McMath had a propensity for the spectacular on and off the course and the personality to pull off such flair. He was known for his unique holiday cards and included his caddie on his Christmas list every year, with a generous bonus included. In one card McMath, the "distinguished" Bethlehem Steel V.P., was elaborately dressed as a court jester. Another featured a tuxedo-clad McMath with his wife in a gown dripping with jewels (of course) toasting each other with martinis from Casa Mia, their winter home in Florida. Though the Christmas bonuses have long been spent, today Cotton still has the cards that spill out of his overstuffed, memory-laden scrapbook.

In 1955, McMath learned that Cotton's daughter Dolores, who was a newlywed and recent high school graduate, was looking for a job. Bypassing The Steel's long waiting list, he immediately offered jobs to both Dolores and Lou, her new husband. Dolores held an administrative position, which included long hours of delivering mail from department to department, all the while wearing meticulously applied make-up, impeccably coiffed blonde hair and three-inch (or more) high heels. "We wouldn't have imagined wearing anything else," Dolores says. "The women of Bethlehem Steel thought they were hot stuff, and quite frankly, the men agreed." This comes as no surprise considering that New York models were hired to train the Bethlehem plant guides on the subjects of grooming, poise and etiquette. The storied legacy of female workers at The Steel also includes what was known as the "Pistol Packin' Mamas" who actually carried guns and kept watch for plant saboteurs during the war. In order to keep the girls from being trigger happy, The Steel charged them for each bullet used.

One day when Cotton was looping for Steel executives Lewis Foy and Stuart Court, Court teasingly said to Foy (purposely loud enough for Cotton to hear), "Let's just give Cotton a 50-cent tip today." ($5 was customary at the time.) Cotton, getting in on the fun said, "Just give me 25 cents—it's an honor to caddie for you guys." Foy deadpanned to Cotton, "That's a crock of ! # * ! ." Only on a golf course was it likely for three men from such different backgrounds to enjoy this kind of rapport.

Cotton's mood changes from playful to sober when he says, "Mr. Foy is 90 years old now and still lives in Bethlehem. When he dies, he'll be buried near Grace's grave." In the shadow of the behemoth and iconic remnants of the Bethlehem Steel (the company survived Grace by 43 years), Cotton sometimes visits Nisky Hill Cemetery and sits at Grace's grave. Sitting under its rotunda on the semicircular granite bench that seats up to 20, Cotton talks to him about old times. "But I get to do all the talking now," Cotton jokes. Underneath the laughter, Cotton seems to be reflecting on something deeper—as if he is bidding adieu not only to the last of the "Men of Steel" but also to a bygone era.

Similarly, when Cotton visits his wife, Florence's gravesite, he'll wander around looking at the names of people for whom he has caddied. "There must be at least 300 guys buried here who I caddied for," Cotton concludes with a sobering appraisal, "The hands on the clock don't stop for anyone."

The legendary steel tycoon and golf aficionado,
Eugene Grace, September 20, 1953

Eugene Gifford Grace (1876-1960)
President, Bethlehem Steel (1916-1945)
Chairman, Bethlehem Steel (1945-1957)
Honorary Chairman, Bethlehem Steel (1957-1960)
Honorary Chairman, SVCC (1955-1960)

One of the photograph Christmas cards sent to Cotton
by tuxedo-clad Bethlehem Steel Vice-President Robert
McMath and his bejeweled wife

In the Rough

NOW A VETERAN MARRIED COUPLE, Cotton and Florence's romance had evolved from stomach butterflies to an enduring love that sustained them through the challenges of day-to-day life. It was the kind of love that transcends graying hair and sagging skin. Like most couples who married in the 1930s, Cotton and Florence held to the traditional roles designated to husbands and wives. He brought home the bacon; she fried it up in a pan. Their two-bedroom, one-bath house was a homey little brick Cape Cod on a quaint, residential street in northeast Bethlehem surrounded by sturdy old houses and unfenced yards, laundry flapping on the lines. The sidewalks were bumpy and cracked, the concrete undermined by the roots of towering trees lining the streets. Only those who visited the Young's cozy abode would believe how much like a storybook gingerbread house it was.

No life is immune to struggle, and this couple would not get a free pass from pain. Florence usually avoided doctors, but she was hospitalized after fracturing her leg in 1983. Additional examinations revealed a lump in her breast. A diagnosis of cancer intersected with Cotton and Florence's quiet existence, and it struck cold terror in Cotton's heart. Barbara, the youngest of their three daughters, recalls, "Dad had absolutely no fear about anything that I can think of—except my mom's health."

At 64 years of age, Florence needed to have a mastectomy. Everyone deals with crisis in different ways. Florence, usually more prone to fear, astounded her family members when she took the news in stride. Barbara surmises, "Mom knew for many years that she had a lump in her breast that could quite possibly be cancerous, but kept it to herself. I think it almost came as a relief to her to finally face the fear of the unknown." Cotton, on the other hand, never usually rattled by fear, took the news far worse; he was stunned beyond belief. "This was the news I dreaded hearing, in some way or another, all of my married life," Cotton lamented. Consumed with chaotic thoughts and frightening scenarios, overwhelmed by decision-making, and completely exhausted, Cotton pressed on to support his wife in whatever way he possibly could.

With Florence being the first in the family to have breast cancer, it was an eye-opening experience to learn of the alarming statistics issued by the National Breast Cancer Foundation: "One woman in eight either has or will develop breast cancer in her lifetime. Every twelve minutes a woman dies of breast cancer." Thinking of their wife, mother or grandmother in terms of these statistics was unimaginable for the family.

Florence bravely faced her leg surgery and mastectomy. She was laid-up for quite some time with a cast that stretched from her ankle to her hip. Cotton still keeps the tattered piece of paper from 1983 in his wallet with "January 21 to February 9" written on it—the dates of Florence's extended hospital stay. Confident they had eradicated all the cancer, the doctors didn't recommend follow-up radiation or chemotherapy treatment. This recommendation would later be brought into question, but at the time Florence knew that youth and beauty were fleeting and the removal of her breast did not devastate her. She was just grateful the cancer was gone.

Although sadness and depression is often a normal part of the breast cancer recovery process, Florence maintained relatively good spirits. Without going through the debilitating process of radiation or chemotherapy, Florence didn't experience the same kind of weakness and fatigue that most women do during their recuperation process. With the surgeries behind them and a clean bill of health for Florence, the couple once again returned to the cozy comfort of home and the quiet life they had made for themselves.

It's normal for any cancer survivor to wonder, "Will it come back?" Florence was no exception. According to the National Cancer Institute, "the five-year survival rate for breast cancer that has not spread to other parts of the body is 80 percent. Newspaper and television reporters usually translate this to mean, 'You're a survivor if you've made it five years past the initial treatment.'" So, after five years, Florence and her family thought she was free and in the clear to take her place as one of the fortunate and brave who have survived breast cancer—a priceless gift as the couple's 50th anniversary approached.

Cotton still clings to the golden memory of that special day in 1987 when he and Florence, along with their family, celebrated their silver anniversary at the

Smithville Inn in New Jersey. Treasured memories include the couple tenderly feeding each other "wedding cake" as their favorite Anne Murray love song, *Can I Have This Dance?* played in the background. The events of the day offered sweet flashbacks to days gone by, like first falling in love, the birth of their three daughters and purchasing their homes together. Cotton's happy recollection of that day strengthens his voice and animates his gestures. To him, these memories are priceless.

In 1993, Florence's prognosis would change. Her cancer had returned and this time it struck with a vengeance. Exactly 10 years after her original diagnosis, the merciless disease had found its way into her bones and liver. In fact, it was so advanced that Florence chose not to undergo chemotherapy and radiation. According to a nonprofit organization for breast cancer education, www.breastcancer.org:

> When cancer comes back, it is a regrowth of the original cancer, previously thought to be eradicated or in remission. In other words, cancers from other parts of the body rarely spread to the breast or the chest wall. If you have metastases to the lungs, liver, bones, or brain, it is more likely to have come from the original breast cancer than from a new and different cancer.

> It's hard to make sense of this diagnosis, particularly if your original cancer was completely confined to the breast (with or without lymph node involvement), and your chest X-ray, blood work, and bone scan were all normal and your surgeon assured you: 'I got it all.'

This is exactly what happened to Florence, leaving Cotton both thunderstruck and terrified by the implications for his wife. Speaking of their last weeks together triggered a rush of memories and left Cotton in a subdued mood. He still winces when he thinks of the pain Florence suffered. "I never saw someone with such a high tolerance for pain, and yet she never complained," says Cotton in a meaningful blend of sympathy and admiration. All the while, Florence's pain cut through his heart and soul like a knife.

As they waited for the inevitable, Florence's family left the world of small talk and current events and entered the place where life stops and time stands still. Cotton's bedside vigil seemed to go on for a small eternity. With a feeling of helplessness, he took a quick break in St. Luke's hospital cafeteria—the very hospital where all three of his children were born. From across the table, Cotton's daughters, Barbara and Pat, were startled at how pallid their father looked in the overly bright hospital cafeteria. His eyes appeared even bluer than normal. Unsuccessful at keeping anxiety at bay, he couldn't stop his mind from drifting to thoughts of Florence and how life would be without her. Cotton slipped in and out of quiet, reflective dazes, often too choked up to speak. The only time his family ever heard Cotton voice even one regret about his chosen course in life is when he wondered if, had he been a man of greater means, he could have done something more to help his wife. He turned to his daughters and asked with pained expression, "Would it have mattered if I had more money to get better medical care?" Barbara and Pat lovingly reassured him that the doctors were doing everything they could. This deeply human moment is forever etched in his daughters' minds.

On August 18, 1993, Florence slipped away peacefully. The extraordinary, intangible presence we call life was gone. After 56 years of marriage, Cotton would not easily overcome the pain of a broken heart.

Normally Cotton is very private when it comes to expressing his emotions, so when he barely eked out the words, "She was the only woman I ever loved," through sobs during the funeral service, it was an especially poignant moment. The depth of sorrow in in his voice spoke volumes. Both the words and the way in which he uttered them jumped out and clutched the heartstrings of every person within earshot, producing a domino effect of emotion.

The well-meaning attempts of family to comfort Cotton seemed woefully inadequate. With unmitigated grief and churning emotions, he sought a quiet and private place to agonize. Nobody really knows what Cotton did for the rest of that day, but it's likely he cried his tear ducts dry.

Family members were there to help with all the funeral arrangements, to comfort and support, and write thank-you notes, but inevitably they drifted back to their own lives. In his aloneness, Cotton was left pouring just one cup of coffee, setting one place at the table and looking for someone else to tell the stories, observations and jokes he would have normally shared with his wife. Life just wasn't the same for Cotton without Florence, in countless major ways, and all of the small ones.

Every young bride and groom dream of living happily ever after, but that dream ended when Florence died. Life as Cotton knew it was altered; he couldn't yet see nor grasp what lay ahead. The stark emptiness of the house haunted him at times. By fulfilling small household tasks, filling up the refrigerator, replacing light bulbs or changing the sheets, the grieving husband attempted to recreate the same warmth voided in Florence's absence. To no avail.

For a season Cotton remained in an awful state of mind, feeling disconnected, alienated and isolated from the very things that made his life worth living. Though his heart was in shambles, over time he began experiencing momentary diversions from the sorrow. These diversions helped ease the ache of this consequential life passage and while the road back to living life was a hard one for Cotton, he knew that the greatest challenge was accepting that his path must now be walked alone.

By nature Cotton isn't prone to melancholy. So, shoving his grief aside, he eventually picked up a bag again, threw the strap over the middle of his shoulder and with purposeful strides walked down the greens of the Old Course as he had many thousands of times before. Florence's death, like his father's, disrupted everything. Golf once again was his refuge and the path forward from personal tragedy. He chased the game to fill his days and buffer his grief. Things made sense on the course. The curative powers of returning to looping helped him outdistance the loss of his greatest love and the pain that restrained him. Through his years of playing and observing the game,

Cotton had learned that sometimes the only thing left for one to do is to accept the inevitable bad lie and continue on. And so he did.

2005 marked the 12th anniversary of Florence's death. Had she lived, the couple would have been married 67 years. Someone asked, "Did you ever think of marrying again?"

"Never."

As the present fades into the past Cotton hesitates momentarily, allowing his voice to fall to a whisper, "She's *still* the only woman I ever loved."

Cotton and his one and only love, Florence

Celebri-Tees

TO COTTON, GOLF HAS ALWAYS BEEN more than a game—much more. It's a personal link with history, and with the interesting personalities the game engages. Since the day he first started strapping on a bag, many golf clubs have changed hands from faithful caddie to famous player. Cotton recalls with remarkable clarity the high points of a career that brought him in close contact with experts from every field in life.

Golf levels everyone, even the rich and famous. Although Cotton has caddied for dozens of famous people, it was never his way to be star struck. Perhaps that's why he was so well received by celebrities—he never asked for an autograph or photograph or made a fuss, striving instead to protect the coveted privacy most stars forfeit for fame.

When asked privately, Cotton will disclose dozens of the prominent names he's met on Saucon's courses over the years. The professional and amateur golfers represent a veritable "Who's Who" in the chronology of the sport...from Sam Snead to Byron Nelson, Ben Hogan to Bobby Locke, James Thompson to Chi Chi Rodriguez, the Golden Bear himself, Jack Nicklaus, and gallery favorite Arnold Palmer. He carried the bags of Philadelphia amateur Woody Platt (who Cotton witnessed shoot a 66), one-time caddie and 26-time PGA tournament winner Henry Picard, 1957 Masters Champion Doug Ford and Dave Marr, winner of the 1965 PGA Championship. Marr was PGA player of the year in 1965 and was later appointed Captain of the 1981 Ryder Cup team.

Cotton considered it an honor to loop for Chick Evans who learned to play golf while he was a caddie. He reached the highest point of American amateur golf by being the first to win the U.S. Amateurs twice, once in the same year he won the U.S. Open in 1916. The only person to duplicate his feat since was Bobby Jones in 1930, the year of his Grand Slam. Because Evans chose to maintain his amateur status, he directed all monies he won to be put into a scholarship for caddies. Today, his dream lives on through the Chick Evans Scholarship Program for Caddies, which has been sending deserving loopers to college since 1930. It's the largest privately funded, sports-related scholarship program in the world, with more than 8,000 alumni. Chick had a special place in his heart for caddies, and Cotton says, "Caddies have a special place in their hearts for Mr. Evans."

In 1922, Gene Sarazen, at the age of 20, became the youngest PGA Champion. When he captured the 1935 Masters, Sarazen won the *career* Grand Slam— all four of the professional major tournaments. (Since then only four other golfers have duplicated the feat: Jack Nicklaus, Ben Hogan, Gary Player and Tiger Woods.) In the final round of that tournament, the "Squire" hit the most famous shot ever in major championship golf, holing a 4-wood from 225 yards away for a double-eagle 2 on the 15th hole. This shot, reputed to have been "heard around the world", helped put the Masters tournament on the map.

Sarazen shaped the future of golf in 1930 with the invention of what is considered to be the first true sand wedge, which he debuted at the British Open in 1932. He envisioned the concept while watching millionaire Howard Hughes work the controls of an airplane. The sand wedge revolutionized the game, dropping average scores dramatically and bringing about the remodeling of golf courses.

From the first moment Cotton met Gene Sarazen, he felt a certain kinship for the legendary golfer. Cotton says, "He was a fast player. No long pre-shot routines. He'd decide on a club, step up, hit the ball and move on." In Cotton's mind, Sarazen holds the distinction of being the "nicest" pro he ever caddied for, bar none. Maybe it was because he was a caddie-turned-player. Perhaps it had something to do with their similarity in height and build (Sarazen was the shortest of golf's greatest champions at 5'5" and weighed just 145 pounds), or the way Sarazen putted cross-handed. Possibly it was Sarazen's personal crusade to double the size of the hole on playing fields (every duffer's dream) or the fact that the early golf hero also dropped out of school at a young age to help support his family. But most likely, it goes back to the legendary and heartwarming story of Sarazen and his caddie, Skip Daniels and the 1932 British Open which actually began in 1928.

Golf great, Walter Hagen and Gene Sarazen were making the voyage across the Atlantic to compete in the British Open. Hagen, the idol of Sarazen's youth who was to become the rival of his prime, had won the championship two times before. Sarazen was hungry for victory, and told Hagen, "If there's any one thing I want to accomplish in golf, it's to win the British Open. Hagen informed Sarazen that he'd never win without the right caddie. Because Hagen had won the championship two times before, he offered to loan Sarazen his caddie, Skip Daniels.

Sarazen took Hagen up on his offer, and on the eve of the championship, he vowed to "abide by his caddie's advice at all times." Yet when he and Daniels had a different view on how to get out of the tall, thick rough on the 14th, a par-5 called Suez Canal, Sarazen chose his own strategy against his caddie's advice. He ended up with a 7 on the hole. It cost him the British Open which he lost to—none other than—Walter Hagen by two strokes. His gracious caddie's response came in the form of a vow: "We'll try it again, sir, won't we? Before I die, I'm going to win an Open Championship for you."

Four years later, Daniels was an old man when Sarazen returned to his home course of Royal St. George's Golf Club to play in the British Open. By that time, Daniel's speech was slower, his eyesight was failing, and he walked with a pronounced limp. Though Sarazen was emotionally torn, he decided he would be better served by a younger man.

However, during practice rounds, Sarazen and

his new caddie didn't get along and Sarazen decided to swallow his pride on the eve of the championship and ask Daniels, who had refused to carry any other player's bag that week, to carry his clubs. "You won't find me going against your advice this time. You'll be calling them and I'll be playing them," Sarazen promised Daniels.

Four days later, with a score of 283–70, 69, 70, 74–13 under par, Sarazen and Daniels won the championship together. Unprecedented at the time, Sarazen asked the officials if Daniels could come up and stand beside him as he received his trophy, signifying it was a team victory. Though they regretted to turn him down, having a caddie share the limelight with the winner went against tradition. Daniels stood among the crowd during the presentation ceremony proud to have made good on his promise to win Sarazen the championship. Skip Daniels died only a few months later.

Roger Penske, Driver of the Year in 1961, also graced the Saucon Valley Course with Cotton on his bag. Penske retired from racing competition a few years later to create one of the most successful franchises in the history of motor sports.

Cotton's caddie repertoire included comic and television show host Woody Woodbury, rich baritone and opera singer John Raitt (famous for his roles in the classic musicals *Carousel and Oklahoma*), entertainer Mike Douglas, dance instructor Arthur Murray, Bob Hope's bandleader Russ Brown...and the list goes on. Working at such a high profile club, Cotton never knew who would show up on any given day to request his services. That mystery was part of the excitement that kept Cotton's occupation fresh for almost eighty years.

The time he caddied for the wholesome American icon, Lawrence Welk is a favorite celebrity story of Cotton's. Best known for his bubbly "champagne music" and the phrases "wunnerful, wunnerful" and "a-one and a-two and a-three," Welk was, at the time, the second richest man in show business after Bob Hope. Yet for all of his wealth and fame, he had the reputation of being tight with a buck. Instead of tipping for services, he was known to hand out penknives inscribed with his name.

Welk was also known as a tough competitor on the golf course—a claim Cotton confirms. At the end of the round, when tipping customarily took place, Welk handed his caddie—you guessed it—a faux pearl penknife. Cotton was unaware of Welk's resistance to tipping, so rather than being disappointed at the lack of a customary tip, he accepted the knife with gratitude.

To this day, he considers it a treasured memento commemorating his day on the greens with "Mr. Wunnerful."

Perry Como—the man Bing Crosby said "invented casual"—was famous for his relaxed baritone vocals, cardigan sweaters, and his love of golf. He and Cotton hit it off right away. Both had easy-going and unassuming manners and both were hometown heroes, born and raised in Pennsylvania steel towns. One of 13 children whose career spanned seven decades, Perry Como was one of the last crooners on the American pop music scene. Though one of the most successful performers of the 20th century, he is often remembered by those who knew him as a deliberately simple man, the man we saw in the Christmas specials, the man who never forgot his roots. Yes, he and Cotton had much in common.

To Cotton, the memories of the day he caddied for the beloved singer still remain fresh in his mind. Como's golfing partner was basketball Hall of Famer Bob Cousy who, during his years with the Boston Celtics, played in 13 consecutive All-Star games, set 13 playoff records and captured six NBA titles. After 17 holes of Cotton's storytelling and expert caddie advice, Como put his arm around him on their approach to the 18th and said, "You are absolutely the greatest!" So taken with his caddie by the end of the round, Como rewarded him with a $20 tip (a princely sum at the time) and an invitation to buy him a beer in the clubhouse. When the last ball dropped into the cup on the 18th hole, however, about 20 Como groupies seeking autographs converged on the star and Cotton never saw the likes of him again. "I guess a bunch of swooning women beat a beer with a caddie any day," Cotton says with a hearty laugh.

Regarding his years at Saucon, Cotton jokes, "I caddied for two Fords and a Lincoln." The famous Fords to whom he refers are former President Gerald Ford and entertainer Tennessee Ernie Ford. And as for the Lincoln—that's Leroy Lincoln, chairman of the board of Metropolitan Life Insurance Company.

Former President Gerald Ford had a reputation for hitting errant shots. He never lived down the time his ball struck an unsuspecting spectator, knocking him unconscious. The unfortunate fan was taken to the hospital, and the newspaper headlines around the country read "Fore! Ford is on the Tee!" Ford's good friend and playing partner Bob Hope often quipped, "Ford made golf a contact sport."

It's not every looper who can claim to have caddied for a one-time occupant of the White House. Even presidents get a thrill from the whack of a well-struck drive. President Gerald Ford (whose birth name was Leslie Lynch King Jr.) took up golf as a youngster, and was a much better golfer than credited. Probably the most athletic of all presidents, he turned down two offers to play professional football. Golfing was said to have been the 38th president's way of easing the pressures of the Oval office, and was criticized when he played golf within days of first occupying the White House after Richard Nixon's resignation.

Though critics opined, "He wasn't a natural at golf or the presidency," Cotton stops far short of calling him a duffer. "He was a long hitter and steady player, and held his own against Mr. Foy (Bethlehem Steel president) and Mr. Busby (president of Pennsylvania Power and Light)." Cotton went on to defend Ford's contribution to golf. "No president has played in as many Pro-Am tours as he has." (Perhaps he was influenced during his vice-presidency with Richard Nixon, who commissioned a golf course to be built next to his home in San Clemente. After Watergate, however, the project fell through.)

In keeping with Cotton's assessment, Gerald Ford once out-drove Arnold Palmer and Gary Player at the first tee during the inaugural PGA World Golf Hall of Fame Tournament at Pinehurst, North Carolina in 1974. His drive measured a whopping 275 yards.

To top that, he has bragging rights to not one, but three holes-in-one.

There were other politicians on Cotton's caddie radar. By a coincidental meshing of circumstances, Cotton now happens to live in the Fred B. Rooney building named after the same U.S. congressman who used to caddie with Cotton.

Cotton also looped for Thomas Dewey, the 1948 presidential candidate and crusader against organized crime. Dewey was so favored over his opponent, Harry Truman, that on the night of the election newspapers around the country printed headlines declaring Dewey's victory. President Truman had the last laugh though, documented in the famous photograph taken the morning after his victory where the President-elect is gleefully holding-up a newspaper with the headline "Dewey Wins in Landslide." This was obviously a crushing defeat for Dewey although, at Saucon one afternoon, he was the master of a dramatic victory. According to Cotton, "Dewey may have lost the race for the White House, but the day he played Saucon's greens he sunk a 40-foot putt to win the round." One can only hope that recalling this unforgettable putt helped to soothe the memory of his election defeat.

Spanning across nine decades, Saucon's courses have not just been sun-kissed, but star-lit. Part of the charm of Saucon is that you can walk the fairways and imagine puring the same tee shot or sinking the same putt as one of these famous players. By all accounts, Cotton extended the same uncommon courtesy and respect for both celebrities and members alike. He reels off the names of every club champion, caddie master and greenskeeper (later called golf course superintendent) since 1929 with as much esteem as the roster of dignitaries and celebrities. Whether carrying bags for the rich and famous or for the thousands of members and guests of Saucon, Cotton gave every player the celebrity treatment. In retrospect, Cotton believes he was able to please them all.

All, that is, but one.

One for the Ages

WHEN SAUCON VALLEY HOSTED the 1992 U.S. Senior Open, Cotton went from relative anonymity to national prominence. During the championship, he caddied for the ageless Jerry Barber. Newspaper headlines read "One for the Ages" heralding the pairing of the oldest active touring professional with the oldest active caddie. One such article, now so faded from age its origin is indiscernible, is still placed prominently in Cotton's scrapbook. The article stated, "At 76, Barber rarely has a chance to play with kids his own age, until now. Barber's caddie at Saucon Valley Country Club is local institution Cotton Young. Young, who like Barber is 76 years old, has been looping at Saucon Valley for 63 years..."

Cotton was naturally drawn to the exploits of Barber whose legend originated from the putts he holed in the 1961 PGA Championship. In that tournament, Barber rolled in putts of 20, 40 and 60 feet for birdie, par and birdie on the final three holes, enabling him to make a comeback from four strokes behind. The next day, Barber shot a three-under-par 67 to his stunned opponent's 68—and at age 45 became the oldest PGA winner. "Talk about a show of long putts," Cotton remembers, shaking his head back and forth. In 1961 alone, Barber won seven PGA Majors (only five are counted today), was Captain of the Ryder Cup Team and "Putter of the Year."

While golf addicts are propelled by the blind optimism of improving enough to shoot their age even once, Barber holds the record (estimated at over 300) for "shooting his age or better." In 1962, he made a hole-in-one at the Buick Open in Flint, Michigan, which is believed to be the first ace captured on film. Barber also pioneered the use of the sand wedge from the fairway, laying it back and using it as a lob wedge before such a club was actually invented.

It was Open week at Saucon and life was good. When Cotton saw Arnold Palmer, Jack Nicklaus, Gary Player, Lee Trevino and Chi-Chi Rodriguez on the practice greens at the 1992 U.S. Senior Open, he said, "It doesn't get any better than this." The legendary five helped to attract galleries totaling more than 150,000 that week; a crowd larger than Cotton had ever seen at Saucon and up to 1992, the most ever to witness a Senior Open. In the rarefied air of the championship, the collective tension of that many mute, motionless, enthusiastic golf fans waiting to burst was a feeling like none other. Because of his age Cotton knew that this could very well be the last major championship in which he could caddie. It would be a defining sports moment for him—his last chance to participate in an event alongside the very best in the world. Unfortunately, golf nirvana was not to be in the cards for the raring-to-go caddie.

Those in the know say that the trouble started when Barber reserved a Saucon caddie but instead showed up with his own. Cotton just so happened to be the caddie on reserve for Barber. Too late to pick up another bag, etiquette would, at the very least, dictate that Cotton should be paid for the week's work. Saucon Valley Country Club, known for its professionalism, held Barber responsible to do just that. In response, a reluctant Barber opted to employ the Saucon caddie as he originally promised. Cotton, no stranger to getting along with his players under all sorts of circumstances, felt confident he could overcome the ill-fated start by offering Barber his time-honored caddie skills.

"Most of the guys want you to read the greens for them, especially when they're on a strange course," Cotton recalls. After 63 years, Cotton certainly knew how to read Saucon's greens. But in the end, it is always the player who determines how much of a role a caddie will play. "Barber told me on the first practice tee that he didn't want any help lining up putts. He said he's the best there is at reading greens." Reporting on the subject, a newspaper article entitled "Jerry Barber Can Shoot His Age Without Lining Up Putts" by Terry Larimer in *The Allentown Morning Call* read, "Apparently, Barber had no interest in putting together 152 years of experience, deciding his own 76 was good enough."

"To make matters worse," said a Saucon Valley source (who did not want to be identified so he could speak more candidly), "Barber resented sharing the media spotlight with his caddie. Cotton was featured that week in numerous newspaper articles and hounded for interviews including one that ran on ESPN." Fellow caddie Larry Taglang says, "Cotton got more publicity at the U.S. Senior Open than his player did."

Though trim and fit at 76 (Cotton has maintained

the same weight and waist size for over 60 years), the newspaper photos showed Cotton traipsing behind Barber sagging under the weight of his bag. The beads of perspiration that broke out on his forehead had little to do with the heat. Cotton was known for his affability, and even on bad days, his demeanor never perceptibly changed. So when Dolores, watching her father from the other side of the gallery ropes, saw his tense expression, she knew something was wrong.

"Something's up. I never saw Dad look so strained before," she said to her husband. Cotton explains, still grimacing, "I carried two bags, five days a week for 76 years and two of them don't weigh what this *one* did." Barber's bag was the heaviest Cotton had ever lifted, and it had a compartment that the cantankerous old pro warned his caddie not to open. "That must be where he hid the bricks," Cotton says with a chuckle. "My side was sore for two whole weeks." Barber made sure his caddie's lot didn't rise above a beast of burden.

There were a few lighthearted moments in the tournament, though, like when Barber poked fun at Lee Trevino's caddie. As a comeback Trevino quipped, "What do you mean? Yours is so old he caddied for Bobby Jones." The people in the nearby grandstand overheard the exchange and had a good laugh along with Barber, and Cotton, who still guffaws today when he recounts the story.

Apparently Cotton wasn't the only one to have difficulty with Barber. Technically, gamesmanship isn't cheating, but it is a form of psychological warfare. It doesn't necessarily violate the rules, yet may violate the intent of the game, which is sportsmanship. A *Golf Digest* article from June 2003 by Nick Seitz entitled "Wizard with the Wand: Jerry Barber's Putting Display At Olympia Fields In 1961 Still Astounds Those Who Saw It" states:

> "He had a chip on his shoulder, being little," Bob Goalby says. "A lot of guys didn't like him because he played hard. And he could drive 'em crazy getting up and down from everywhere. Then if he did something a little off-color, it got to 'em…" Goalby says, "We called him Little Caesar." He'd say, 'I'd rather be a little bleep than a big bleep like you …'

> Arnold Palmer and Doug Sanders criticized Barber at a senior event in Charlotte, N.C., for standing too close and moving while they putted. "If you're trying to constantly psych somebody out," Palmer said at the time, "that's not in the spirit of the game, and you shouldn't do it." Barber vigorously disputed the contention.

As for Barber's game at the Senior Open, he shot a
74-75-76-74 for a 299. As usual, Cotton was right and
the Old Course humbled the arrogant player. Barber
missed putt after putt on its treacherous greens. To
further quote from the article "Jerry Barber Can
Shoot His Age Without Lining Up Putts": "He hit
every fairway, but his putter failed him [Remember,
he was renowned for his putting.] and he took 34."
Most of the world's top golfers concede that their
tournaments boil down to putting contests and in
most instances faulty alignment is the culprit. "You
can't just outmuscle the Old Course, you have to
outsmart it," says Cotton, holding back a smile. This
is a statement that is unmistakably Cotton.

Much was made of Barber continually shooting his
age, and rightly so, but one wonders by his behavior
if he acted his age. Haunted by the putts that got
away, Barber was more interested in winning the big
money than in shooting his age. If he had taken some
of Cotton's advice he may have taken a larger portion
of the $2.5 million Senior Open purse.

The winner was dictator-sized, cigar-chomping
Larry Laoretti (who is reputed to rarely take a waking
breath that isn't filtered through a cigar*) with a
flawless final round of 68. His four round total was
275, nine under par and four shots ahead of runner-up

Jim Colbert. Jack Nicklaus, who shot a 67, turned in the best round on championship day. Other highlights included 12 players shooting 33 on the front nine, two players shooting 31 on the back nine and four players shooting 66 for the best 18-hole score.

After seven days of backbreaking work (three days of practice rounds and four tournament days), Barber wanted to compensate his caddie with a meager $400. Cotton insisted that this was far below a fair wage, and Barber begrudgingly conceded to part with $500.

The 1992 U.S. Senior Open remains the single biggest disappointment of Cotton's career. Many would suppose that he would harbor a dislike for Barber. But Cotton, who rarely utters an unkind word about his players, allows for only one comment while shaking his head, "He's a tough man." Though the prediction came true—the 1992 U.S. Senior Open would be Cotton's last major championship—he determined not to let one negative experience color a lifetime of positive ones.

*In *Golf Magazine's* April 2005 issue, Josh Sens writes in an article about "Golf's Lost Arts": Sometimes a cigar is just a cigar. And sometimes it's a swing aid. Former U.S. Senior Open Champion Larry Laoretti, who has nary swung a club without a stogie clenched between his teeth, tells you how a cigar can help you smoke your shots. 'It's not rocket science,' he says. 'If you want to hit it straight, put the cigar in the middle of your mouth. To hook it, hold the cigar on the left side. To slice it, the right side. Simple as that.'

The Express-Times / Peter Paolicelli

1992 U.S. Senior Open

Hole-in-One

GOLFERS RARELY FORGET THE FIRST TIME they hit a golf ball well. The lure of golf is the magical way the ball flies through the air. If you hit a pure shot everything within yearns to duplicate the experience. Inexplicably, repetition never diminishes the yearning.

When Cotton is asked why golfers forsake family and friends, put in hours and hours of practice on the driving range and spend $630 million just on golf balls alone every year, he hesitates momentarily as if there were just too many reasons to limit himself to a concise reply. His best attempt at an answer is two-fold: "On the course, golfers can leave their problems behind. Golf can have that effect on players, maybe because it creates so many new ones [problems]," Cotton laughs out loud. His second observation is: "It only takes one really good drive to get hooked."

It's true. Without a 12-step program, once a golfer is hooked, his fate is sure. And every time a golfer places a tee in the ground he's asking for trouble—and all too often, on all but the best days, calamity chases him. (We have a Scottish shepherd who struck a little rock into a rabbit hole with a shillelagh to thank for all this.) Though the odds aren't in their favor, all golfers still dream of the day when they can mark an ace on their scorecard. According to *Golf Digest Magazine*, that dream comes true once in every 8,000 shots—all the more reason for golfers to get out on the course as frequently as they possibly can.

The *first* known hole-in-one recorded in a tournament was in 1868 at the Open Championship at Prestwick, Scotland. History was made when Old Tom Morris scored the ace on the 145-yard 8th hole.* The *oldest* person to ever mark a hole-in-one on his scorecard was Harold Stilson. His record-breaking shot occurred when he was 101 years of age at the Deerfield Country Club in Florida. He died less than a year later—a happy man. Lastly, the *most* hole-in-ones to be recorded was a mind-boggling 49 made by golf pro Mancil Davis.

Over the course of his illustrious caddie career, Cotton witnessed two aces on the Grace Course's 3rd hole. There were, however, extenuating circumstances surrounding one of the magical shots. "This story is as hard to believe now as it was then," Cotton remarks. The tale of Dr. Bruce Kaufmann's famed shot will appeal to the fortunate few who have had the exhilarating experience of making a hole-in-one, and to those who long to join the ranks of this elite group.

The trees arrayed in their autumn finery of crimson, orange and gold, marking the arrival of October, often brought a bittersweet feeling for Cotton. The beginning of October signaled the official closing of another golf season. The game of golf thrives on its variables which include but are certainly not limited to skill, club selection, course design and weather conditions. As far as weather goes, blue skies and warm temperatures are preferred by most, but to some, playing in freezing temperatures adds an extra element of adventure to the experience. For fair weather golfers late autumn may be the end, but not for a certain group of Saucon's die-hard golf devotees who are known to play winter golf now and again.

Casting off their three-month-wintry-weather-sentence, Bruce Kaufmann, Jim Knicos and Russ Kopy, believed there was no better way to greet the New Year than on Saucon's frozen links. It would serve to strengthen resolve in their New Year's resolutions which were largely comprised of bettering their golf games. "There's a sort of charm to playing golf in the dead of winter," says Jim Knicos.

It was January 1, 2000 and a balmy 15 degrees—in other words, a perfectly good day for golf. The course was deafeningly silent, the only sound the whistling of wind through naked trees. The grass looked beaten down and forgotten. Most of the wildlife had long since gone south to flee the Pennsylvania chill, and the rest of nature was in its annual slumber. Though the cold wind made it difficult to hold steady over putts, the white knuckled players nevertheless persevered. Cotton was accustomed to caddying in the muggy, heat-drenched summer, but in deference to the blustery winds and frigid temperatures, he wore long thermal underwear, layers of sweaters, gloves, a hat and a hefty winter coat. Filling the chilled air with little white puffs of golf course banter, the players and their caddies made their way over to the third hole of the Grace Course (one of Saucon's three courses remains open all year round).

With a wind-assisted wallop, Kaufmann blasted a

strong drive down the frozen fairway. No one would have guessed the trajectory of Kaufmann's ball as it soared toward its intended target, showing no sign of weakness. Cotton says, "The ground was so hard it was like playing on concrete." The ball bounced and bounced and bounced and rolled over the frost-burned turf, honing in on the flagstick as if guided by a global positioning system (GPS), and then disappeared. From the tee, it looked as though Kaufmann might have shot the ball down the par-3, 210-yard hole for an ace! The group was momentarily shell-shocked until someone broke the silence and finally said, "Let's go check the hole." Anxious to confirm the one-shot phenomenon, they hurried toward the flag. Kaufmann was the first to peer into the hole. A smiling Titleist was staring him back in the face. Incredibly, his ball had found the hole.

According to Jim Knicos, the Golf Channel reported that Kaufmann's ace was the first hole-in-one *in the world* that year. The extraordinary shot proved how quickly lightning can strike in the game of golf, even in the dead of winter.

Part of the charm of golf may be that success sometimes comes just because you're out playing the game. That thought alone is enough to give a hacker hope. Conversely, it is also the nature of golf to withhold reward from even the most perfectly executed shots.

Listening to and telling one golf tale after another is part of what makes the game so special. For most people, their golf improves in retrospect, and thus, their stories are known to get better and better in the telling and retelling—just like the fish that got away is always quite a bit larger than the one that makes it home for dinner. But there's no need to embellish this story; it's too much like a tall tale to be one.

The dapper caddie still freighting two bags in his
golden years on Saucon greens.

Caddie Immortality

AFTER A SUMMER DAY of looping in 1999, Larry Taglang returned to his van in the sweltering heat to discover a mysteriously placed *Orlando-Sentinel* newspaper article on his windshield. "How could a Florida newspaper end up under my wipers in Pennsylvania?" he pondered to himself. It was especially unusual because his minivan was sitting in an isolated parking area where caddies leave their vehicles during peak golf season. A van shuttles them to the caddie shack from there. (To this day, he is beset with curiosity about the origin of that fateful newspaper article.) Giving it a cursory glance, Taglang noticed a headline reading, "The Caddie Cause." Exhausted from 36 holes of looping, he mistook the article to be about *tour* caddies, which didn't concern him, because he was a *club* caddie. The article unceremoniously landed in a pile on his back seat.

It wasn't until many months later that Taglang's eyes fell upon the newsprint again, and this time he read its entire contents. Realizing that the Professional Caddies Association (PCA) was searching to honor both tour *and* club candidates for their years of distinguished caddie service, he immediately thought of nominating Cotton and surreptitiously did so. "I kept it a secret—no one knew. Not Cotton. Not even the club. I patterned my whole life after this guy," says the towering Taglang. "I figured he was a shoe-in!" Rather than be intimidated by his friend's notoriety, Larry admired it and didn't hesitate to call the PCA and request the necessary forms to submit Cotton's nomination for the Hall of Fame.

The two had met while working for Bethlehem Steel and caddied together at Saucon for nearly 40 years. Both men possessed an unflinching work ethic. One record-setting winter storm rendered car travel impossible in the Lehigh Valley, but did not keep Cotton and his friend, heads bent against the blustery wind, from walking to their shifts at The Steel. The sharp, biting force made a mockery of their face scarves. The entire town was engulfed in a shroud of snow, yet being lone travelers in the severe weather did not deter them. "Cotton and I were among the very few to show up," says Taglang.

By mid-morning, the treacherous Nor'easter's blast was tallied in feet, not inches, when the shift foreman came up to Cotton, instructing him to "punch out at 11 o'clock to get his four-hours." According to Taglang, this didn't sit well with Cotton. "He was a nice guy; but he was no pushover. Cotton could be tougher than a one-iron if he thought it was necessary. He figured if we walked to work in a blizzard, we should at least get our eight hours that day." Cotton never went looking for trouble, but when trouble showed up, he responded. With steely resolve (if you'll forgive the pun), Cotton took up the cause for both he and his friend; all it required was one phone call to upper management. Minutes later, the contrite foreman walked up to the two men and said, "You can punch out at three," guaranteeing that their trek through the snow would garner them a full day's wages.

Further evidence of Cotton's favor with The Steel's upper management, according to Taglang, "is when the foreman would deliver a message from number three man Robert McMath to Cotton at the beginning of his 7:00-3:00 shift to meet him out at the club just before noon." Taglang laughs, "The real kicker is the foreman was instructed to pay him for the full eight hour shift in addition to his caddie pay. Cotton may not be very tall in stature, but in my eyes, he's always been ten feet tall." Cotton had a personality that belied his height.

From The Steel to the fairways, these caddie comrades are bound together with a lifetime of experiences. "Often, Cotton and I were assigned loops together, and we would wait for our players to arrive at the first tee," says Larry. "On many occasions, when a member would bring guests for a round, introductions would be made and the guests would reply, 'Cotton, your reputation precedes you.' What a compliment!" exclaims Taglang. Anyone who ever played the Old Course without having Cotton as a caddie really missed out. I was all ears when I was with him, taking mental notes about how he got along with the players and his stories about each hole and the club's history. Then I'd repeat the stories to my players, and they were always fascinated by them."

Nearly five months later, Taglang finally got the phone call confirming that Cotton's nomination was accepted. He couldn't wait to announce the news to his long time mentor and friend.

It was March 2000, and Cotton was waiting for

the bitter Pennsylvania winter to give way to the early blush of spring and with it the revived hopes of golfers and caddies everywhere. The uneventful passage of time was interrupted by the shrill ring of the telephone. "Cotton!" a familiar male voice called out, boisterous with excitement. Larry was on the line, and this was no ordinary phone call. "Pack your bags," he announced to Cotton with palpable delight. "You've been accepted as an inductee into the Professional Caddie Association's (PCA) Worldwide Hall of Fame." Cotton fell silent. For a moment, time seemed to be at a standstill, as if his mind was overloaded with the enormity of the honor. Taglang eventually broke the silence, and for Cotton, who had never been airborne, the next bit of news added to the excitement. "You'll be flying all the way to the World Golf Village in St. Augustine, Florida as a guest of the PCA.

Escorting Cotton from Saucon Valley was fellow caddie Kevin Nicolas, who was assigned to capture the three-day event behind the camera's eye—a special provision paid for by the staff and members of Saucon who took up a collection to pay Kevin's way. It was appropriate that Larry Taglang and Peter Fidorack ("The first Saucon caddie to ever own a car," Cotton says, "And co-winner of Saucon's 1939 Best Caddie

Award with me.") drove the pair to the Philadelphia International Airport, sending them off with celebratory fanfare.

Cotton's daughter, Dolores, was just returning from a month-long trip to Florida when she received the phone call from her father with the exciting news. Expressing her congratulations with an equal mix of laughter and tears, Dolores also conveyed her regret. "After just returning from Florida following an extended vacation, I couldn't possibly take additional time off to attend the ceremony," she told her father. Cotton understood—but he should have known better. Dolores wasn't about to miss a once-in-a-lifetime opportunity to celebrate such a high point in her father's career. She quickly made arrangements to return to Florida in time to surprise her dad the night of his arrival.

Aside from a couple of memorable vacations master-planned by daughter Dolores and her husband, Frank, Cotton had rarely been south of the Pennsylvania state line, and had never boarded an airplane. As he was about most things, Cotton was fearless when it came to flying, but approached the experience with childlike wonder. The plane was nearly full leaving only a few extra seats. Cotton walked down the narrow aisle and sat in a seat by the window.

As the flight attendant gave instructions on what to do in the event of an emergency, Cotton as a first-time flyer wondered why no one else paid attention.

That day in the air a spectacular sky was on display. The sights below grew smaller and smaller, and he was reminded of the miniature landscape of Bethlehem's Moravian Putz. The scene was ever changing. At first the piercing blue was embossed with fleecy white clouds drifting peacefully through the sky. Then it was brilliantly sunny above a cumulus awning, swallowing any sight of land. One minute the colors were opalescent; the next, the huge orb of the sun would drench the clouds with hues of pink and gold. The flight was over much too quickly as the pilot rode a tailwind into America's Sunshine State.

One highlight of the whirlwind trip was the 2000 Liberty Mutual Legends of Golf tournament at the Slammer and the Squire at the World Golf Village. In 1978, this inaugural event, representing senior play at its best, sparked the creation of the Champions Tour, formerly known as the Senior PGA tour. That first year, Sam Snead and his partner, Gardner Dickinson, stole all the headlines and won by a 12-stroke margin of victory, taking home the $100,000 purse. Since then Lee Trevino and Mike Hill have won the tourney a record-setting four times.

Among the players in 2000 were Tom Watson, Jack Nicklaus, Chi-Chi Rodriguez, and Lee Trevino. After finishing second twice in this tournament, Jim Colbert teamed with Andy North to finally win the event. Cotton announces with the finesse of a television sports broadcaster, "North made par on 17, and Colbert sank a 4-foot putt for par on 18 to seal the win."

From the stands, Cotton had a panoramic view of the unfolding drama on the course. With all the "legends of golf" on hand, he was surprised when autograph seekers at the 18th hole sought *him* out to sign their programs and hats.

Another highlight of the three-day trip came during the 2000 Caddie Cup, a match-play event with the *Senior* PGA tour caddies vying against the younger PGA tour caddies for the cup. In this competition pitting the wisdom of experience against the vigor of youth, the *Senior* PGA tour caddies won hands down. Least surprised by the outcome was Cotton.

The night of the induction ceremony was March 19th. The Renaissance Hotel at the World Golf Village set the scene and a red carpet was rolled out for the venerable old caddies. Among Cotton's contemporaries and Hall of Fame inductees were:

- Willie Peterson, Jack Nicklaus' caddie
- "Creamy" Carolan, who caddied for Arnold Palmer,
  Ben Hogan, and Sam Snead
- "Tip" Anderson, Palmer's caddie for 35 years including the
  year he won the British Open
- "Rabbit" Dyer, Gary Player's caddie with 30 wins in six majors
- "Killer" Foy, Hal Irwin's caddie with 49 years on tour
- Jim Clark, Baltrusrol Golf Club's 90-year-old caddie and
- Freddie Bennett, caddie master at Augusta National.

It was as if a golf time machine swooped down from another era. Some of these vintage caddies began their careers in a time when players still requested a mashie, spoon, or niblick for a club. Can you imagine what they might think of the SmartSwing driver with computer hardware imbedded in the shaft? This technology provides players with detailed feedback on the intricacies of their swing, storing the information in the club's memory. How times have changed, but with all the advances of technology, the perfect swing remains elusive. And while the advances in equipment are fascinating, so are the marked contrasts in caddie demeanor since "the good 'ole days." These caddies, schooled in the gentler courtesies of the game, are still likely to doff their hat in respect to ladies. Wouldn't it be interesting to hear them "weigh in" on one prominent tour caddie who threw a fan's camera into the lake? True, the fan was careless and the shutter excruciatingly timed, but the venerable caddies would likely be horrified by such a lack of temperance.

When a white stretch limousine arrived to transport him to the ceremony, Cotton said, "Look at the size of that thing!" Not familiar with the protocol of such luxuries, Cotton made his way to the front of the limousine only to be gently guided to his place in the back. After years of Cotton driving his players in golf carts, it was his turn to be chauffeured as a guest of honor.

The induction ceremony was a high-spirited event unlike anything Cotton had ever experienced. In every conceivable way, it marked one of the true highlights of his life and career. Included in the festivities were silent and live auctions with proceeds benefiting the PCA's mission to "...provide its members, caddies, their families and others with additional income opportunities, high quality benefits, services and certification through educational and communication programs world wide...and to bring back caddies and preserve the tradition of the game of golf."

It was a heart-tugging moment when Cotton saw

the hearty thumbs-up signaling that it was his turn to speak—a moment that exhilarated this man of simple dignity. The excitement Cotton felt was only marred by fleeting thoughts of his beloved Florence. What would she make of all the hubbub surrounding her husband?

Cotton seemed small behind the microphone-laden lectern, backdrop of festive banners and presence of PCA leaders—that is, until he began to speak. Nobody would have blamed him if he proved a reluctant raconteur. After all, he was 84 years old in an unfamiliar setting. But from the moment he took his place at the podium, he was humorous and relaxed, completely at home behind the microphone. Unmoved by the spotlight, he lapsed into the wonderful state of simply being himself. Never even considering the need to jot down notes, he spoke straight from the heart about the subject he loves the most. His delivery was as warm and homespun as a fireside chat, and the audience was captivated.

An analysis of Cotton's acceptance speech doesn't have to separate stagecraft from substance, because there was none of the first and all of the second. He never lost the caddie's common touch so his diction wasn't flawless, but the moment was genuine. He leaned into the podium and in his quaint way revived the tales that displayed the heart of his caddie career, many of which are contained in the pages of this book. This was Cotton at his best. When finished, he bathed in the applause that erupted with approval, accepted the congratulations, and quietly walked off stage. Dolores, who enthusiastically joined in the ovation said, "As his daughter, I couldn't have been more proud."

Laura Cone, PCA President, would later make a trip to Saucon—experiencing for herself the enchanted backdrop of Cotton's caddie career. In front of Saucon's classic Georgian red brick clubhouse, she ceremoniously presented Cotton with a Waterford clock and official PCA Worldwide Hall of Fame banner to the sound of clicking camera shutters.

Cotton's contributions as a caddie have been well documented over the years in numerous newspaper and magazine articles. Scores of these yellowed clippings provide glimpses into his life, their headlines serving as the mile markers:

- Fountain Hill Golf Champ Honored
- Young has Caddied for Two Fords and a Lincoln
- Packin' the Bags
- Caddie Still Carrying Clubs at 76
- Sitting Pretty
- At 76, Caddie Still Reads a Mean Green.

After Cotton's induction into the PCA Worldwide Hall of Fame, Hubert Pedroli and Mary Tie Green included him in their book *1,001 Reasons to Love Golf*. Found in the chapter on "Legendary Caddies" with the subheading: "Part craftsman, part advisor, part companion, caddies carry much more than bags on their shoulders," Cotton is listed as the 808th reason to love golf! It reads: "Ross 'Cotton' Young has caddied for Saucon Valley Country Club for over 71 years."

Infused with the optimism that comes on the threshold of a brand new golf season, Cotton's return from Florida coincided with one of his favorite events of the year—Opening Day at Saucon. The morning temperatures in early spring of 2000 were still chilly, yet the daytime warmth was enough to set in motion Saucon's impressive show of budding trees all on the verge of green. It was a teasing but unmistakable hint of summer's reluctant approach. The Saucon creek shone platinum in the spring sun.

Though Opening Day tourneys are for *members only*, Cotton was invited to the official kick-off of the golf season and introduced to the membership as if he were a "two-legged historic landmark." His many years on the bag rightfully made him a club treasure. The introductions were followed by breakfast with the members, then a round of golf and lunch. Season after season, year after year, decade after decade, Cotton's face is the face that many Saucon members have associated with the country club. In fact Cotton's values and work ethic have become synonymous with the tradition and professionalism that defines Saucon. In Ralph Grayson Schwarz's book, *Saucon Valley Country Club- An American Legacy 1920-2000*, Schwarz says of Cotton, "Saucon Valley Country Club has been the beneficiary of distinguished and dedicated professional leadership over the years and with competency and loyalty through the ranks. Ross "Cotton" Young is such a person. He continues to serve as a caddie today, in the eighth decade [now in his ninth] after he first came to the club as a caddie in 1929 at the age of 13..."

But this year Opening Day would hold an unexpected surprise. Upon seeing Cotton, members initiated an unscripted, two-minute long standing ovation. The spontaneous, heart-warming tribute almost brought Cotton to tears. Desperately trying to cope with the lump that was building in his throat, Cotton looked out at the crowd, for a moment seeming to retouch his youth. He started playing golf at Saucon when he was a kid, immediately fell in love with the game, and never looked back.

Golf had been his work-and-pride ever since. Cotton genuinely felt his service contributed to the well-being of Saucon members. Of all the honors over the years, few tributes touched Cotton more because, in a tangible way, their affection for him seemed even deeper than he had previously known.

The members and staff of Saucon would break tradition again and invite Cotton to the *member's only* Christmas party in 2003. Weeks earlier, Director of Golf Gene Mattare nonchalantly asked Cotton what his favorite hole of the Old Course was. Without hesitation, Cotton's reply was "the 15th!" That night the holiday crowd presented Cotton with a beautifully matted and framed picture of the 15th hole that is now proudly displayed in his living room. Gene Mattare, whose kind acts still stand out in Cotton's memory, thoughtfully carried the large picture to Cotton's car for him.

In golf, as in the rest of life, winning is better than losing. But win or lose, it is especially rewarding when you can be proud of how you made your way along the course.

Caddying provided a heritage on which Cotton's name could be engraved. From rookie looper to caddie pantheon, he will be forever immortalized in the Professional Caddie Association Worldwide Hall of Fame. Yet to Cotton, his greatest achievement was winning a place in the hearts and memories of Saucon members. He says, "Some members are like family to me," which is more than a figure of speech for Cotton.

Rare is the legend that is remembered as much for the sincerity of his personality as for the many accomplishments of his career. Combined, these made Cotton not only a great caddie, but also an even better person. When all the scores are totaled, his legacy as a man may add up to the greatest tally of them all.

Being interviewed by a reporter for the Golf Channel,
the evening of his induction into the Professional Caddie
Worldwide Hall of Fame

Cotton and PCA Founder Dennis M. Cone

With his fellow Hall of Fame inductees

From left: "Rabbit" Dyer (Gary Player's caddie with over 30 wins
in six majors), Cotton, Sam "Killer" Foy (Hal Irwin's former
caddie with 49 years on tour), Jim Clark
(Baltrusrol Golf Club's 90-year-old caddie)

Acknowledging his acceptance into the
PCA Hall of Fame and regaling the crowd
with his engaging fairway tales

Cotton's face in repose during the PCA Hall of
Fame Induction ceremony has the solemn dignity
of a man 72 years on the bag.

Staying the Course

GOLF IS TRULY AGELESS. Unlike any sport, golfers can—and do—swing a club into their 60s, 70s, and even 80s. The golf ball doesn't distinguish the age of the person who hit it. While the grace of the greatest of games is that golfers can often participate into old age, the bodies of average golfers cannot tolerate extended periods of *good* golf. Though some golf swings mysteriously survive longer than others, the magic eventually wears off.

Cotton hasn't actually *played* golf in years, so he jokes about his game. "The older I get the better I was." Cotton knows that his best golf is in his rear view mirror; a fact that he accepts, as his lifelong goal was to lower the handicap of others rather than his own.

For Cotton, age is usually something to enjoy—even to laugh about. "I'll die young at an old age," he says, half-jokingly. "And that's not just a play on my last name." There is a deeper truth behind his words. The unspoken subtext reveals that Cotton truly has gone through the latter part of his life feeling like, on the inside, he is still in his 50s. Though he has the same physical expectations he had more than 40 years ago, his body says otherwise, and young people often perceive him as ancient. Cotton's internal, seemingly never-ending reservoir of youth continues. His internal clock may have grown wiser but not older. Sometimes it startles him to look down and see the hands of an old man. They are still useful hands, but there is no denying they are the hands of an 89-year-old.

Fairway activity has always energized him, and retirement from The Steel, Cotton decided many years ago, was not for resting. Though he has maintained a vigorous, age-defying lifestyle in his golden years, at the age of 82 Cotton finally relinquished a few concessions to senior citizenship. Most notable was downgrading his carry from two bags to one, and eventually the practice of using a cart.

Golf carts were originally designed with the elite, the elderly and the handicapped in mind. Most golfers would agree with Cotton that walking the course with your golfing buddies enhances the game. It is one of the most inherently pleasant aspects of golf, and Cotton's motto has always been, "Walk, don't ride, until you have to, because the less you walk, the less you'll be able to walk." Cotton speaks from experience, having caddied with no major health concerns until he was 88 years of age. It was during one exceptionally hot summer in 1998 that Gene Mattare, director of golf at Saucon, suggested that Cotton use a cart. At first, he fought hard not to, but today, Cotton is especially grateful for the privilege. He is the first and only caddie at Saucon to have been given the opportunity to drive a cart to compensate for advancing years.

Though Cotton continued to loop for the members and guests of Saucon, he did not caddie for the 2000 U.S. Senior Open. He accepted this verdict of time, rendered because he could no longer walk fast enough to keep up with the pros in a major tournament. It was strange for him to see bags on the back of the other caddies and not his own, yet Cotton's "celebrity" had not diminished. *The Allentown Morning Call* ran full color advertisements for their special golf sections entitled "Senior Open Preview" and "Saucon Valley Hole by Hole" where Cotton shares his insights on each hole of the Old Course.

Bill Killian sent Cotton a ticket to the Open, and an invitation to dinner following the tournament. For Cotton, it would be his first chance to enjoy the extraordinary atmosphere of a U.S. Senior Open solely as a spectator. Excitement was in the air. The grandstands were packed, and the greens were surrounded by galleries ten-deep that raced for position to watch every shot. Everywhere Cotton looked, there were people. The Old course had taken a beating by Mother Nature that week, leaving her vulnerable and defenseless. "Thunderstorms late Thursday and Friday made the greens soft and fast. There wasn't even a breeze to contend with," says Cotton. "It was as if the course was only made up of fairways and greens. The players were making every shot." For once, par didn't seem as precious a score on the Old course.

In the same year that Tiger Woods posted a staggering four round total of 12-under-par in the U.S. Open at Pebble Beach (the first in a 100 years of U.S. Open history that a player shot a double digit number under par), record scoring turned the big scoreboards into a sea of red at Saucon. In a tournament typified by a dazzling flurry of birdies, Hale Irwin's 17-under-par win beat the record by three strokes.

Runner-up Bruce Fleisher tied the previous record at 14-under par, and Jack Nicklaus shot a 67, which tied his best round in any Senior Open. (The Golden Bear won this championship in 1991 and 1993.)

All this record scoring begs the question: Do the galleries enjoy a birdie barrage or would they rather follow after players hacking their way around a course? "With few exceptions—like Arnie's hair-razing comebacks out of the sand—crowds would rather be bird-watching than biting their nails any day," Cotton says.

According to a July article, "Saucon's Proud Old Course Peppered But It Was Fun Watching The Birdies Fly" by John Kunda in *The Allentown Morning Call*, Tom Kite defended the Old Course with this endorsement: "Saucon Valley is a wonderful test and I hope that the USGA doesn't hold these low scores against it. It's a shame the rains came. Other than that, golly, everything was first rate. The volunteers were super; the crowds were large and enthusiastic. This is a wonderful venue for the Senior Open. I hope we come back."

During the day, Killian recalls running into Cotton, who was furtively dodging an interview with an ESPN reporter. When Killian asked Cotton why, he replied with furrowed brow, "They want to interview me with Gary Player's caddie, Rabbit. At 6' 6", he's almost a foot taller than me. A guy has to have a little pride. I don't know what all the hoopla's about, anyway." (What is all the hoopla about? Might it be that you caddied for 72 years and, by God, you earned some?) The reporter and his film crew never did find Cotton. Perhaps he was faster on his feet than previously mentioned!

Four years later, at age 88—his energy not resembling his age—Cotton, the product of Pennsylvania's Steel Belt and a depression-bred toughness, was amazingly still caddying the first weekend of April. Two days later at home, without warning, his right hand suddenly started tingling and he had difficulty breathing. When he began to have trouble talking, his speech noticeably slurring, he became concerned and drove himself (much to his family's chagrin) to the hospital. The doctors confirmed that he had suffered a stroke. He would undergo two operations—one to unblock the carotid artery on the left and another on the right side of his neck. Having a number of complications and a few scares, his hospital stay totaled 14 days.

Afterward, Cotton was of smaller voice and vacant look. This was to be expected so soon after a stroke. He changed after conquering his brush with mortality. Cotton seemed to revisit the past to look for that thing, whatever it is, that gets lost on the path from childhood to adulthood. It's that intangible thing that has been known to return to those who choose to age gracefully. No longer was a squeaky front door considered an affront to the proper way he should maintain his home. Rather, it was viewed through new eyes as an easy way to know that someone who cares has arrived for a visit. Cotton became more apt to focus on the essentials and less on the peripherals. With a fresh appreciation for the gift of life, fewer extraneous details bogged him down. This is best revealed by his response to daughter Dolores' request for his Christmas list. Cotton's reply? "Just more time to visit together."

In the weeks following his stroke, Cotton offered another hint at surrender. Although Barbara and her husband Eucline (who live in nearby Easton) faithfully cared for him, the thought of shoveling the snow, mowing the lawn, trimming the bushes and keeping up with household repairs became too much for Cotton. With surprising ease, he made the decision to move into an assisted living facility. With far less ease, family members struggled with the decision, but they eventually supported it. After all, 872 Hilton Street held years of memories to which their hearts were tied. They would leave behind the kitchen where Nana served chicken potpie and the basement where pool on the miniature billiard table was played. Christmas cards would no longer line the banister and the comforting presence of Pop-Pop sitting in his favorite easy chair near the front door would pass forever.

People face retirement at different stations on the time portal, and certainly Cotton had defied the odds. While golf has an irresistible, almost addictive power over golfers, the same is true for this caddie. Cotton claims the fascination rests much less on its physical challenge than the way the game engages the mind. Those caught in its clutches say that golf isn't a game, it's a bondage. In 15th-century Scotland, golf was banned for a time by the King, because golfers had become so obsessed with the game that they neglected their archery practice and thus undermined the country's national defenses. (Not much has changed, as any golf widow will attest.)

What is it about caddying that is so appealing to Cotton? As stated, the love of golf is a large part of the equation. His great love for the members and staff at Saucon is another. But an additional part stems from the sensibility that his life was good because it was lived from his roots, where his values provided a source of energy, enthusiasm and direction each day.

Aside from being deprived of his family, losing the ability to loop would be the worst thing in the world for Cotton. Since Florence's death, he begged little more of life than the opportunity to continue. Though faced with considerable physical challenges, it wasn't long before Cotton began expressing his lofty goal, "I hope to get my caddie legs back in a hurry." Call him tough. Call him tenacious. Call him a dreamer. But don't, Lord knows, call him finished.

Since caddying has been the substance of his life, the day Cotton no longer feels able to will be a dark day indeed. Chick Evans once said of Walter Hagen, "He's in golf to live—not to make a living." The same could be said of this lifelong looper. Cotton maintained that he would caddie until he died.

Skeptics who doubted his ability to caddie again were clearly unfamiliar with his limitless determination.

Jack Nicklaus, Arnold Palmer, Hale Irwin, Tom Kite and Tom
Watson are portrayed in front of SVCC's Signature 18th Hole.
The commemorative print *"The Legends of the Millennium"* cap-
tures the essence of the 2000 U.S. Senior Open Championship.
(Charles P. Vlasics, Artist, 1999)

Love Me, Love My Caddie

DURING COTTON'S RECOVERY from his stroke, Gene Mattare encouraged him to come regularly to the club for visits with members and staff. Aging Saucon members who rarely play the course themselves viewed Cotton's desire to continue looping as nostalgic rather than hopeful. Others, particularly golfers for whom Cotton still caddied, rallied around him at this crossroads. Cotton devotees, bolstered by their affection, remained optimistic that he could once again loop.

Jim Knicos, owner and president of Nicos Polymers & Grinding, Inc., 10-year member of Saucon Valley Country Club and card-carrying golf addict is one such man. He and Cotton share an extraordinary relationship, best explained in Knicos's own words:

When I first met Cotton in 1995, all I saw was a white-haired man, a caddie, in a golf cart. I asked someone, "Who's that?" They replied, matter-of-factly, "He's Cotton." By the manner of their response, I felt like surely I should have already known that.

My curiosity was aroused. "Who is this caddie driving around with golf clubs and not carrying bags? What's so special about him? Why would a caddie be allowed a cart?" It seemed contradictory, but whenever I asked why, I always received the same reply: "He's Cotton." My fascination grew.

Not until he finally looped for me would I grasp exactly the legend of this person nicknamed Cotton. That chance came a whole year later in 1997, when a member he was supposed to loop for didn't show. Why did my wait endure so long? Because the list of golfers who requested Cotton as their caddie was long—and my name fell at the bottom of the list.

On that fateful day, Cotton met me out at the first tee. He was meticulously dressed, clean-shaven, every hair fastidiously in place; his clothing washed and neatly pressed—a pattern I would learn he repeated every day of his long career. His presentation reflected a personal dignity that impressed me, and beyond appearances, I began to admire this caddie as a person.

Cotton and I made a special connection our very first time out on the course. He was respectful, mannerly and his looper skills were second to none. This master of his trade could skillfully dispense yardage, read greens, proffer sage advice and keep me from losing my cool during particularly tense times— just by his very presence.

From that day on, I always requested Cotton to loop for me, and it eventually became an unwritten rule. For new club members who asked the question, "Why is that caddie in a cart?" my reply now echoed the others. "He's Cotton."

With a reputation for an outstanding work ethic preceding him, this consistent and disciplined caddie always showed up a half-an-hour early for his loop. It has been said that up until his stroke in 2004, he was never sick a day in his life. I never saw him miss a day of looping due to illness—and he usually played every day he could for most of the year—weather permitting.

Cotton had a particular grace about him. While the rest of the world seemed to be on overload or in a hurry, this was not true of Cotton. He knew who he was and was secure and comfortable in his own skin. I wondered at how a man could be so completely content. Somehow, life seemed to be, for him, simpler than for the rest of us. Clearly, this was a man who thoroughly enjoyed what he was doing—perhaps more so than some club members with wealth, high-powered careers and impressive titles.

He may never have bought a luxury car, lived in a million dollar home or experienced an extravagant vacation, but he enjoyed what no amount of money could purchase—the priceless gift of true contentment. No, Cotton may never leave his family a sizable inheritance as measured by some, but who could put a price tag on his legacy of honor?

Cotton is a lovable old man. In the absence of my grandfather and father, he became a bit of both to me. He would never presume to call me his friend because of his insistence on protocol—but I am proud to call him my friend.

Though at times (especially after a bad round) I may have given up my golf game, Cotton never gave up on me as a golfer. He suffered along with me through my bad shots and reveled with me on the good ones, mastering the balance of remaining positive and supportive without being patronizing. Although, the comedic possibilities are broad, given the ball's knack for finding places that were not intended for its presence, I never saw Cotton laugh at one of my poor shots.

Unique to the sport of golf is this amazing bond between two people, golfer and caddie. Though two-player sports do exist (as in doubles tennis and beach volleyball) the difference in golf is that the caddie is not a player but rather a type of assistant, allowed to be right in the thick of things. We played as one, in perfect synchronicity. I could sense Cotton's body tense until my shot was hit. His support of me was palpable. "I'm rooting for you" seemed to be an invisible banner he held up over his head.

Don't think for a moment that I was the only one to enjoy a celebration or bragging rights. Cotton seemed to feel the swell of pride just as strongly as I did after a good round. He could often be overheard giving others a stroke-by-stroke replay, boasting about me to people who could obviously care less. Players generally enjoy the spotlight and Cotton never minded their shadow.

We are close in an unspoken way. We just always understood each other; a rare quality in any type of relationship. When I made a bad shot, we'd look into each other's eyes and then back down to the ground again. Yes, we had an understanding.

Cotton could say more in three minutes than most people could in three hours. We've never had deep conversations, but rather spurts of honesty in our times together. It has been said that you can't hear what some men are saying because their actions speak louder than their words. For Cotton, the opposite was true. His actions spoke the loudest and most of the time words just weren't necessary.

He never intimidated a golfer and, at the same time, was never intimidated by a golfer. A scratch golfer would receive the same care and attention as would a 40-handicapper, if Cotton was the looper.

This man, my caddie and friend, is an authentic human being, possessing the dignity and class that accompanies accepting one's station in life. In fact, he is not only comfortable, but proud of who he is. If more were like him, this world would be a better place. Cotton is an inspiration and makes me want to be a better person.

The most colorful view of the game of golf comes from the caddie, who has an exclusive window into this world on the greens and is privy to on-course dramas not often revealed to just anyone. Who knows a golfer better than their caddie? Who witnesses them each minute of every round, hears their muttering and intimately knows their strengths and weaknesses? Cotton saw all kinds of men over the course of a 77-year career. Some were morally weak; some were cons. Never influenced by the dark side, his "caddie honor" would not allow him to even acknowledge, much less repeat, an impropriety—even if decades had passed.

From all over the course, it was not uncommon to hear ladies yelling out greetings to Cotton, who was particularly popular with the female members at Saucon. I began to tease Cotton, saying, "What's this about the members' wives?" Cotton didn't catch on at first, but then emphatically replied, "Oh no, Mr. Knicos. Oh no!" This became a long-standing joke between us. In later years, Cotton would reply to "Are you chasing the members' wives around again?" with, "It wouldn't do me any good if I caught them."

As our relationship grew and we both got older, I would tease Cotton saying, "You're walking like an 80-year-old!" Incidentally, Cotton was 88 at the time. This is a man who, at 78, started a decade-long tradition of running from hole 13 to hole 14 as a forecaddie, running on ahead of his player to spot the flight of the ball. Cotton took advantage of the opportunity to get additional exercise and keep fit. Upon his departure, I'd yell, "Don't get lost!" to which he always replied, "I'll try!"

Cotton is given the run of the country club now. He's like the unofficial mayor. You can find him riding his cart down the sides of the fairways with everyone from greenskeepers to members waving a hearty greeting.

Just as Cotton championed my cause for years, on and off the course, I hope to champion his cause now as he makes the transition to being less active on the fairways.

No caddie ever rode in a cart at Saucon before, and no caddie will ever do so again. Of course, no one person is bigger than the club itself, but Cotton is and will always remain a Saucon institution. He's a living legend.

After all, "He's Cotton."

On one of Cotton's visits to Saucon, the grand 'ole caddie emerged from the caddie shack, crossing the parking lot with momentary, uncommon vigor. His stride was almost youthful when he caught a glimpse of Jim Knicos. They smiled fondly, shook hands and for a long moment exchanged nods that acknowledged the emotional juncture they had reached. Words alone could not express how each man wished to walk the course together again. Those accompanying Cotton were moved by the power and poignancy of the of the silence. Finally words were exchanged. "I miss caddying for you," Cotton said in a near whisper. "I miss it too," Knicos said solemnly. The words were brief and simple, yet they spoke volumes in significance. Player and caddie caught each other's eye with an intimacy neither man was certain he wished to accommodate. Then Cotton turned away from Knicos and the beloved Old Course that yet remained just beyond his reach.

Several months later, in December of 2004 Cotton did beat the odds and caddied for Knicos once again. He slipped his lean, 89-year-old frame out of the cart, his movement no longer as nimble, a man who bore the scars of the physical strain of his age. Though still handsome, sporting his silvery asset (making him the envy of every middle-aged member with a receding hairline), he appeared wizened and weathered. His blue eyes watered with age. His legs sometimes betrayed him, tired with the weight of his 89 years. Not expecting his caddie to commandeer the cart, Knicos was surprised when Cotton drove up behind the wheel talking animatedly with his golfing partner, Russ Kopy. "He even got out there to rake the traps that day," Knicos exclaims.

Though Cotton may be a little creaky, he will

caddie until he can caddie no more. When failing eyesight betrays his acumen for reading the greens, when he can no longer lift his player's bags, he will still have the admiration and affection of Saucon's members to keep him in the game.

Cotton and his cherished player, Jim Knicos

The Final Fairway

COTTON STILL GETS OUT on the Old Course to "caddie" now and again—addicted to the sight of the fairway, the fellowship found on the links, the sound of the ball hitting the clubface and dropping into the hole. On one such day Cotton ran into Jim Knicos and the rest of his foursome. Here's the account told from Knicos's point of view:

"It was the 4th of July, 2005 and my foursome had just teed off to the par-3, 9th hole on the Old Course. I hit my ball to the green about 12 feet from the hole. As I was crouched down attempting to read the putt, someone said to me, 'Here's Cotton.' He was making his way over to say hello to me and the rest of my foursome: Russ Kopy, Bruce Kaufmann, and Kevin Pennington."

" 'Nice shot,' he said, to which I replied jokingly, 'Thanks. Now let's get to work and help me read this putt. Do you remember how?' Cotton smiled, stood a little taller, and walked a little more sure-footed over to my ball. He looked at it for a whole three seconds and said, 'It's going left at first and then back to the right. Hit it straight on.' I tried to see what he saw, but couldn't. My instinct was to hit it for a right to left putt, but I knew better than not to listen to Cotton—after all, he's Cotton."

"I hit it exactly the way he read it, and guess what? The ball fed perfectly into the cup for a birdie. I turned, looked at him, and he looked at me, just like the old days. I pointed at him and said, 'You are still the best there ever was!' When our eyes met over his successful read it was like Don Quixote and Sancho Panza out for another ride together. It was truly a great moment, and fitting that it took place on the 4th of July—because Cotton can still produce some fireworks."

Even after having a pacemaker placed in his chest at 89 years of age, Cotton doesn't have the sense that his caddying career is over or yet complete. And he's right. People say there's no good news anymore, but here's a hefty dose: yet another honor is to be bestowed on Cotton. Saucon Valley Country Club plans to officially dedicate its caddie shack at a ceremony during the 2005 Member-Member Labor Day weekend tournament, replete with a commemorative plaque to be hung on the exterior of the building in his honor with the inscription:

Ross "Cotton" Young
Memorial Caddie Yard.
Dedicated to our friend Cotton Young
In recognition of his years
of service to the members of
Saucon Valley Country Club.

From then on, perhaps by the time you read this story, it will be known as the Ross "Cotton" Young Caddie Clubhouse. Cotton plans to go 18 holes with Jim Knicos and Russ Kopy in the tournament following the ceremony.

Saucon's intent to dedicate the caddie shack to Cotton was announced at the Stag Dinner, part of a major four-day annual event held in conjunction with the 43rd Annual Norborne Berkeley Memorial Member-Guest Tournament. Cotton was invited to attend the June 2005 dinner as a guest of honor; the only caddie ever to darken the doors of such an event. (The invitation was also extended to me, the VIP's granddaughter—the only woman ever to darken the doors of a Stag dinner and a lone female in a crowd of 200 blue-blooded sons of the game including tournament players and Saucon staff.) Though the announcement was intended as a surprise, the strength of the caddie rumor mill prevailed. Cotton, however, protected the anonymity of his source.

As dapper as ever, Cotton sported a pale yellow suit jacket with a striped tie and shoes so shiny you could almost see your reflection. Dressed impeccably and ready early for his big night, his doorbell rang announcing a visit from the publisher of a local golf magazine seeking an interview for a future cover story highlighting the veteran caddie. An hour and a half later when talk turned to a photo shoot at Saucon, Cotton became restless. With a lifelong reputation for punctuality to maintain, Cotton was ready to make the oh-so-familiar trip to the club.

The festive evening began with a raw seafood bar and drinks on the Old Course putting green in front of Saucon's main classic Georgian-style clubhouse. Cotton got out of the car and was immediately surrounded by members offering their congratulations and a cold beer. Those still under the impression that the honor was a surprise for Cotton desperately tried to curtail the hearty congratulations, which were showering him from every direction.

Though Cotton's movements can now be somewhat labored at times, he was strangely buoyant, operating under the spell of a mysterious grace while players called out:

"Cotton, you're the greatest!"

"There's never been another caddie like you!"

"Will you go nine holes with me tomorrow?"

Hearing the clamor of so many caddying requests was, for Cotton, as satisfying as when he was able to fulfill each one. Colorful fairway anecdotes starring Cotton filled the warm, summer air. One member was overheard exclaiming to another, "Cotton knew how to put a club in his man's hands. To have Cotton by my side was worth a few strokes every time."

Another animated member explained to his guest "Cotton is living history and his stories have become the stuff of legend."

One more of Cotton's players laughingly recounted the time he asked his caddie what his secret to longevity was. Without reservation, Cotton quipped, "Not going to doctors!" This was especially humorous to this particular golfer, because he is a doctor.

As the sun slowly made its descent over the Old Course, a bagpiper in full dress played traditional Celtic music on his journey up the fairway. The skirl of the bagpipes as a musical backdrop instantly identified Scotland, the birthplace and Eden of golf, adding a touch of tradition and drama to the special occasion.

Eventually, the crowd made its way to the Main Ballroom, and Cotton was escorted to a table in front next to the podium along with family members, Saucon staff, Jim Knicos and a magazine reporter searching for a scoop for his next article. The room was filled with fraternal laughter, boisterous and buzzing with tournament players swapping stories of golf and life.

Director of Golf Gene Mattare welcomed those assembled and invited the minister of The Central Moravian Church in Bethlehem, Reverend Dr. Douglas Caldwell, to open the evening in prayer. The minister was also a participant in the tournament, pairing up with his twin brother. Unsuccessful at quieting the energized crowd, Rev. Caldwell jokingly suggested that perhaps those who were still talking would like to come up and join him to pray. A holy hush suddenly descended on the crowd.

Members of Saucon's board of directors stood in the back of the room, anticipating Cotton's recognition. George Burke, Jr., Saucon's club president, read a moving biography of Cotton's life and career. The tribute reached the heart like a one-iron, and was regularly interrupted with enthusiastic applause culminating in a standing ovation when the plan for the caddie shack memorial was at last announced.

Jim Knicos watched Cotton's response to the speech with obvious satisfaction, for he had been a strong proponent of the honor. Cotton was characteristically grateful for the attention, and his face in repose had the solemn dignity and quiet pride of a man satisfied with a life lived well. The old looper sat quietly taking in all the adulation as if it were nourishment to his soul.

When asked if he would like to say a few words, Cotton readily accepted the handheld microphone with the same calm, on-course demeanor for which he is known. He looked out through the crowd with his soft, blue eyes, the eyes that served witness to so many defining moments of golf at Saucon. His voice held layers of feeling—gratitude, humor, and pride.

He began by thanking the members for "putting up with him on the greens for 77 years," followed by a nostalgic look back at his first day of caddying in 1929. He ended with, "I'd tell a few jokes but my granddaughter is in the room." The joke about not telling a joke drew laughter from the crowd.

The meal that followed was fit for a discriminating carnivore, with a generous, man-sized portion of aged prime N.Y. Strip taking center stage. Wine glasses were filled with an ample pour of Pinot Noir. Cotton, however, never managed to eat more than a few bites as dozens of members visited his table during dinner to offer their congratulations. When he wasn't busy receiving a heartfelt thank-you or a pat on the back, Cotton was looking around making certain he conversed with everyone.

Cotton had plenty of company down memory lane that night. Saucon member Jim Singleton was overheard telling the story of Cotton caddying for him during a member-guest tournament a decade or so ago. Here's the scene: Cotton tapped the flag on the green two times as if he were transmitting some hard-won wisdom indicating where Singleton's partner should putt. When the defiant guest player stubbornly perceived he had a better strategy, Cotton just walked away. As the ball missed the hole by feet, not inches, Singleton said to his partner, "Cotton's caddied for 60 or so damn years at Saucon. Who do you think can read a putt better—you or him?" It was a rhetorical question answered only with a crestfallen face. Similar story lines with different names and dates were repeated throughout the night.

"Cotton knows the best angles off the tees, and knows just where to place approach shots into the greens," said a long-time club member. "No caddie will ever navigate a golfer through Saucon's courses any better."

One guest of the club approached Cotton with obvious wonder. Extending his hand, he said in an emotional tone, "You don't know me, but your story humbles me...it humbles me. Thank you." Another passing member commented, "Because Cotton was so unapologetic for who he was, he summoned something of the same in me." These brief exchanges stood out as deeply genuine.

If given the opportunity for more than one round in the fairway of life, Cotton would undoubtedly choose his fairway dreams all over again. Though he was a looper, Cotton went beyond the narrow bounds of his profession in many ways. What may only be a game to some was to Cotton a life's labor. He makes the enviable claim, "I have the best job in the world!" with a look in his eyes that makes you believe it actually *is* the best job in the world. And for Cotton, it is.

Caddies were first called loopers, because they worked in circles. They went out, came back in— and when they finished, they were right back where they started. This lifelong looper transcended the definition of a caddie, for his circles on the greens produced tiny ripples, like a skimmed stone on a placid lake that slowly reached each person he met.

Old age for some can hold a measure of uncertainty and isolation with only the memory of great deeds long past and mostly forgotten. In a time when the number of rounds Cotton caddies has greatly declined, his players haven't forgotten him. Rather, his contributions seem to have become more significant with the passage of time. Just as the tradition at Saucon remains strong as it draws near its second century of history, so too has Cotton etched historic lines into Saucon's caddie ledger. Evidence of his legendary status will be showcased forever at the caddie clubhouse dedicated in his name along with the Ross "Cotton" Young Caddie tournament, already played annually as a tribute to the lifelong looper.

Cotton Young represents the American proletariat—

the Everyman who walked the fairways at Saucon to become a golf folk hero. As he approaches his 90th birthday celebration that will appropriately be held at Saucon Valley Country Club, his legacy continues. 2005 marked Cotton's 77th year at Saucon, his career outlasting the tenures of six greenskeepers, 28 caddie masters and four directors of golf. Still boasting his shock of white hair, Cotton has maintained a lifelong fervor for the game of golf. As popular as ever, his very presence casts a noble air over the caddie profession.

In the golf game of life, Cotton is inarguably an ace. Applauded for his honor, envied for his caddie skills and loved by all, Cotton is a living legend…and the legend continues.

Acknowledging the Ross "Cotton" Young Caddie Clubhouse
dedication at the 43rd Annual Member-Guest
Tournament Stag Dinner

Top left to right: Gene Mattare, SVCC Director of Golf
and George Burke, Jr. SVCC President; Bottom left to
right: Jim Neitzel, Eastern Pennsylvania Golf Magazine
publisher and Jim Knicos, SVCC member

Afterword

Cotton's life is a gift to me and my telling of it is my gift to him. I desired the recollection of my grandfather to be more than sepia-tinted photographs on onion-skinned pages in a tattered scrapbook. Writing *Lifelong Looper* humanized my grandfather. I came to love and respect him not only as my grandfather, but also as the man, the caddie, the husband. The hundreds of hours spent capturing both Cotton's public and private sides, the details of his homespun wisdom, the laughs and quite a few startling discoveries—like the time I learned that my 18-year-old grandfather had been jailed for a week after the Model T Ford he was driving in with three of his friends was mistaken for one used as a get-away car in a bank robbery. Who knew?—were deeply gratifying in ways I could never have predicted and changed me in ways that I am yet to fully understand.

For my family, Cotton, the patriarch and star of every holiday gathering, is the bridge that connects our past with our future. His life as a caddie is not his sole heritage. Looking around at the blond-white tufts capping the heads of his grand and great-grandchildren, you see engraved in them Cotton's indelible mark. I feel as though I'm standing between two generations—one that has started to fade away and one that has yet to begin. I wanted his life story to be preserved and cherished as a reminder of all we owe him and all that we can learn from him. It is my hope that *Lifelong Looper* will be a tribute to aging and a link for future generations to the grandfather they never knew, but of whom they will always be a part.

"To live in the hearts we leave behind, is not to die."
—*Thomas Campbell (1777-1844)*

With his granddaughter and author of *Lifelong Looper*,
Cindy O'Krepki

Acknowledgments

Books are always collaborative ventures, and this one is no exception. Though it's my job to be good with words, it was quite difficult to find the words to thank everybody enthusiastically enough for their contributions.

First of all, thank you, readers, for taking the time to peruse *Lifelong Looper*. Since reading about golf is the next best thing to playing golf, I don't feel so bad about having distracted you from working on your swing for a little while. My hope is that Lifelong Looper will be one of the golf books next to your favorite chair, ready to transport you to the links at the turn of a page.

Thanks to Mr. Arnold Palmer for his graciousness and generosity now added to my long list of his endearing on-course qualities—the pants hitch, lunging swing, bold approach to putting and his final round charges. Long live the King!

Grateful acknowledgement is due Timothy Kling, the consummate professional and creative genius behind our book cover. He captured our vision for the project, and with passion, transcribed it to the book jacket.

The caddies, members, guests and staff of the Saucon Valley Country Club must be acknowledged, for they gave these pages life. Everyone was eager to help. (That seems to be a pattern among golfers.) Doors flew open and stories flowed as soon as Cotton's name was mentioned. My great debt to my Saucon friends is obvious from the frequency with which I cite their experiences. May their reward be fast greens and endless fairways.

One of the great joys of writing *Lifelong Looper* has been the number of new friends it has brought into my life. To Jim Knicos, Myra St. John and Nancy Haldeman I say, "Have angels taken up residence in Pennsylvania?" Generous beyond what I had a right to expect, I thank them especially for the affection they have for my grandfather and their obvious and ongoing support of the book in its many stages.

Thanks to Bill Killian for the immeasurable kindness shown to my grandfather over the years, and for the colorful stories shared about Cotton—not all of which could be used in this book—that cast my grandfather in a whole new light.

Thanks must go to Gene Mattare for his review of various chapters of this manuscript. His sensitivity to the needs of the aging is most touching.

Thanks to Will Harcourt who let *Lifelong Looper* into his life, providing insight and making suggestions on my first draft, when he didn't have room for one more thing.

The manuscript has gone through many permutations, guided principally by Brenda Viola and Sally Branca whose combined suggestions, additions and edits made the book richer than it would have otherwise been.

The keen editorial eye and professionalism of my copy editor, Sally, came to me at a crucial juncture. Like an expert caddie, she gave me the thrust I needed to bring the project to a satisfying finish on the back nine of an unfamiliar course. What began as a literary endeavor between Sally and I ended in friendship and I couldn't be more grateful.

From Brenda's initial enthusiasm about my proposal to write *Lifelong Looper* to her patient editing, she has done more than anyone could expect from an editor. But then she is more than an editor; she is a friend—a friend who lifted more than a few sentences out of the rough and gave them a better lie.

Thanks to my longsuffering friends and family who heard little else than all things "Looper" this past year, and displayed a level of tolerance well beyond the call of duty.

Thanks to my mother and father-in-law for their support through the roughs and hazards of life and writing.

Acknowledgments

When there is good news to share, my mother is usually among the first people I tell, because I can count on her to be as enthusiastic as I am. Her response to *Lifelong Looper* was certainly no exception. Because of her adoration for her father—my grandfather— her heart naturally beat with mine when it came to this labor of love. My appreciation for family was born in her arms, and it was her surge of support in both tangible and intangible ways that continued to move this project forward.

Though many have supported the writing of this book and helped it evolve from my heart to the pages contained here, one must be acknowledged above all others. Without my husband Peter's love and encouragement, I would have never begun, let alone completed this book. He believed in me long before I believed in myself, and because of him, the person I am today is very different from the one he married.

Peter made my writing life possible, encouraging me to unabashedly follow my dream regardless of any personal cost. Not only my rescuer from numerous computer glitches, he also created an atmosphere in our home that nurtured creativity and encouraged excellence. A visionary in my creative endeavors, Peter is also the genius behind the book layout, website design, photography and publishing aspects of writing this book.

How fortunate am I that I married a man so like my grandfather—not because he possesses a cultish obsession with golf—but that he loves me with the same abandon as my grandfather did my grandmother.

References

Grateful acknowledgements are due the authors and publishers of books from which I gleaned relevant material or quoted a few passages. Any errors or omissions are entirely unintentional. If notified, the publisher will be pleased to make any necessary amendments at the earliest possible opportunity.

Forging America: The Story of Bethlehem Steel. The Allentown Morning Call, publisher. Allentown, 2003.

Porter, Penny. *Eugene Gifford Grace- 1876-1960: As We Remember Him.*

Schwarz, Ralph Grayson. *Saucon Valley Country Club - An American Legacy 1920-2000,* Saucon Valley Country Club, publisher. Bethlehem, 2000.

Zullo, Allan. *Astonishing but True Golf Facts,* Andrews McMeel Publishing, Kansas City, 2001.

Photo Credits

Kevin Nicolas

Peter O'Krepki

Saucon Valley Country Club Archives

The Express-Times/photographer-Peter Paolicelli

ABOUT THE AUTHOR

If you had told Cindy O'Krepki that authoring a book was in her future, she may have laughed and dismissed the thought entirely. As a successful entrepreneur in the wellness industry with her husband and partner, Peter, her plate was more than full with one of her life's joys—helping people. A health enthusiast with a passion for the domestic arts, you would more likely find Cindy engaging in adventurous outdoor activity or whipping up a gourmet feast for a party than sitting at a computer, typing words on a page.

Described as indomitable, spontaneous and a gutsy risk-taker, Cindy's love of adventure and travel has taken her to exotic locales like the demilitarized zone (DMZ) between North and South Korea and on excursions like riding the dorsal fin of a shark in the tropical paradise of Belize. Teen years were spent at New Jersey's southern shore and on Southeastern Florida beaches, where her love for all water sports grew from surfing to scuba diving. Cindy continues to gravitate to life near a beach. In fact, the swaying palm trees, sugary sand and ample sunshine of Naples, Florida provided the perfect setting and muse for the final work on this book.

Though a voracious reader, the writing bug captured Cindy as an offshoot of her business endeavors. Seeing a void in marketing materials, she and Peter parlayed their years of experience into two successful coaching publications that continue to sell today. An accomplished motivational speaker, there are many who say of Cindy, "She changed my life."

Cindy's first exposure to golf was her golf aficionado father's putting green on the back lawn of her childhood home. It was the only section of their sizable back yard that was off limits to the kids—that is, unless she and her four siblings were enlisted to help maintain the thick, lush green. From the time golf first started appearing on TV in the 1950s, golf tournaments were the Petras family's entertainment of choice—whether they liked it or not. Her father, now in his 70s still makes it to the green in two.

If there was any hope for Cindy to escape the all-consuming culture of golf, having Cotton as a grandfather sealed her fate. After all, it's not every child who has a caddie legend for a grandfather.

Chronicling the story of Ross "Cotton" Young is the beginning of a new chapter in Cindy's life—one that is richer for having taken the time to mine the gems of life-lessons hidden in the tale of this "Lifelong Looper."